British made?

British

made

Patricia Millard
investigates just how much
British-made is really
made in Britain

Kenneth Mason

FIRST PUBLISHED 1969 BY
KENNETH MASON PUBLICATIONS LIMITED
13-14 HOMEWELL HAVANT HAMPSHIRE
ALL RIGHTS RESERVED
COPYRIGHT © PATRICIA MILLARD
BOOK DESIGNED BY SADLERGRAPHICS
SET IN 10 ON 11 POINT BASKERVILLE AND
PRINTED IN GREAT BRITAIN BY
THE SOUTHERN PUBLISHING CO LTD

CONTENTS

5

*T*o what extent is British industry foreign-owned, foreign dominated, foreign controlled? There is no simple answer to this question, either in terms of finance put into this country from overseas or in the cost to our economy of profits sent abroad. Neither is it possible to assess the benefits that occur to our economic well-being by the introduction of foreign techniques and technologies. What is apparent is that 'British' industry is a vast interweaving of foreign and domestic interests.

This book is an objective study of British industry by market sector to show the extent of overseas investments, both directly in terms of subsidiaries and associates and indirectly by minority holdings, licensing arrangements and the like. The project was attempted because both author and publisher felt it important – and timely – to present the facts on the present investments in industry without emotion and without jumping on any political bandwagon.

Each industry has been considered, as far as possible, in terms of market shares held by companies and all information obtained has been verified by reference to published sources and the companies themselves. At best, market shares can only be a guide to the dominance, or otherwise, of the company concerned but it is hoped that this method of treatment will lend more interest to the subject than a mere listing of companies.

What follows may shock and startle those who are complaisant about British industry today. If it does either, then this book will have served its purpose.

7

I

THE EXTENT OF
OVERSEAS INVESTMENTS

It has been estimated that about £2,250 million of overseas money has been directly invested in British industry, three-quarters of this being American. In terms of people this accounts for some half million workers, about a fiftieth of our total labour force. This compares favourably with Canada where foreign investors, mainly American, own nearly two-thirds of the country's large-scale industry and Australia where non-residents own a quarter. Britain has, however, a higher proportion of overseas investment than her European neighbours. While American investments account for some 17 per cent of British manufacturing industry, comparable figures for Germany and France are seven and five per cent respectively. American investment in Italy is about the same rate as in Western Germany. On the other side of the hemisphere overseas investment in Japan is somewhat hampered by the fact that the government of that country insists on a 51 per cent Japanese ownership.

At least 1,600 non-financial companies in the UK are owned or controlled by American companies. They account for about ten per cent of our total manufacturing sales and their return on both capital and sales is probably 50 per cent or more above the average for the rest of British industry. They are responsible for one-sixth of British manufacturing exports and it has been estimated (Dunning, 1968) that by 1980 between 20 and 25 per cent of all British industry will be owned by overseas interests. Professor Dunning has also estimated that the leading 150 American firms manufacturing in Britain probably account for about 12 per cent of British exports. 1965 figures published by Booz-Allen show that in the period

January to June of that year 386 American companies started 532 foreign business projects including 119 firms who moved abroad for the first time. US companies started 136 new projects in Britain, 11 in Canada, 88 in Japan, 76 in Germany and 66 in France.

The concentration of United States capital lies in the growth or research-oriented sectors of British industry such as those for oil refining, electronics, pharmaceuticals, computers, office equipment and motor cars. These probably account for three-quarters of the total US participation in manufacturing industry.

According to Board of Trade figures, at the end of 1965 nearly two-thirds of overseas investment in the United Kingdom came from the United States and 12 per cent from Canada together making up 78 per cent for North America. The next largest total is for Switzerland, but a substantial part of the investment so recorded probably originated in the United States, the investment being made via a Swiss holding company. Inward investment has been growing at an average rate of 11 per cent a year since 1961, although investments from North America have grown faster at an estimated 12 per cent per year. The highest average rate of growth has been in distribution and investments in engineering industries have increased more since 1961 than those in manufacturing generally.

The greatest proportion of overseas investment is in subsidiaries representing 90 per cent of the total. Eight per cent was in associated companies and two per cent in branches. 82 per cent of inward investment was in manufacturing and 12 per cent in distribution, although a higher proportion from EEC countries (nearly a quarter) was in distribution. In the manufacturing sectors investments can be ranked in size order as follows:

	% of total investment
mechanical engineering	*17*
motor vehicles	*15*
chemicals	*11*
food and drink	*10*
electrical engineering	*9*

A high proportion of investments are of relatively long standing, two thirds of the assets in the UK-owned overseas are in companies established here before 1946. Fresh investments have, however, been numerous in recent years, 44 per cent of the larger and 70 per cent of the smaller investments were established over the past decade. Trade investments in associated companies are mainly quite recent, 62 per cent of these dating from the last ten years. Among the investments dating from before 1939 are those of the American car and tyre companies though these have greatly increased their investment in recent years. A high proportion of foreign holdings in the food and pharmaceutical industries are also of long standing. Fields in which there has been a higher proportion of newcomers since 1946 are textiles and clothing, paper, chemicals and metal manufacture.

Canadian and EFTA investments are largely in the food, drink and tobacco sector with the former having important holdings in metal manufacture and the latter in chemicals. EEC investments are concentrated in electrical engineering (mainly Philips) and in distribution.

Scotland shows a high concentration of US, Canadian and European firms. At the beginning of January 1967, the Scottish Council (Development and Industry) identified 84 American, one Canadian and three European companies operating in Scotland as wholly owned manufacturing subsidiaries. In 1966 North American firms employed just over eight per cent of the total number employed in manufacturing industries in Scotland; investment by North American firms stood at £162 million, exports amounted to £118 million or 24 per cent. The largest group by employment of US firms in Scotland is in the field of consumer durables (including sewing machines, domestic electrical appliances, cookers and electric razors). The principal American manufacturers of office machinery – IBM, Burroughs and NCR have substantial and long established manufacturing activities in Scotland. The third largest group of North American firms in Scotland is in the field of automotive machinery and accessories and includes earth moving equipment, agricultural machinery, industrial engines, tyres and hydraulic equipment. The fourth largest group of overseas investments in Scotland are engaged in the manufacture of a wide range of instruments and electronic equipment.

Overseas investment in Northern Ireland, again mainly American, is now more than $200 million with 35 US companies manufacturing in that area including Du Pont, Monsanto, Ford, AMF, Goodyear and Berkshire.

An overall increase of eight per cent in expenditure on plant and equipmetn was planned for 1968 by the British affiliates of US companies immediately before the announcement of American curbs on overseas capital outflow. According to the US Department of Commerce, the rate of growth of American investments in Britain is slowing down considerably when one considers that expenditure on plant and equipment for 1967 rose by 21 per cent over the previous year.

If the limitation on capital outflow to 65 per cent of spending averaged over 1965 and 1966 was applied rigidly to the 1968 proposed investment, the forecast of £470 million ($1,124 million) expenditure currently on plant and equipment would have to be cut back to £230 ($550 million). The rate of increase has fallen off most markedly in the petroleum industry.

Management today (April 1968) drew attention to the emergence of the multi-national corporation as the dominant economic organisation of the 70's and beyond. Actually the true multi-national corporation scarcely exists; what does exist is the international group, mostly controlled from and owned in the USA, holding major shares of the market in several other countries, an example being ITT which has about one-fifth of its employees based in America and employs almost as many people in Germany and Britain. But the outnumbered American employees used 44 per cent of group assets and generated 46·4 per cent of all sales. General Motors has 16·7 per cent of its total assets but only 14·2 per cent of turnover in operation outside North America. Other American companies in a similar position include Singer, Standard Oil, Caterpillar Tractor and IBM. The scope is enormous. In 104 countries IBM has 331 sales offices, 228 service bureaux, 16 manufacturing plants and six laboratories (in Holland, Germany, Austria, Sweden, France and Britain) each with separate areas of interest. IBM is, incidentally, the world's richest firm with an equity of $35,100 million.

The same trend is happening throughout the larger European companies, Hoechst, Volkswagen, Rhône-Poulenc and Siemens being just a few examples, although hardly any European companies post-war have possessed enough resources to buy their way into large and developed markets on a big scale. The famous European multi-nationals are pre-war in origin and the two biggest, Shell and Unilever, were the result of cross frontier mergers. It should also be born in mind that a substantial part of the equity of Shell, Unilever and Philips is also held in the USA.

The importance of these trans-national companies has been commented on by numerous business economists. Professor Howard Perlmutter has already gone on record by saying that in 20 years' time the business world will be dominated by 300 monster international companies which will have world-wide manufacturing and distribution facilities controlled from headquarters staffed by multi-national teams of executives.

For the present we can only present the picture of industry as it stands today as we hope the following pages will show.

2
EATING, DRINKING
AND SMOKING

Eating is an international pastime and it is not surprising to find practically every sector dominated by overseas investment. The habit is hard to break as almost from our birth the American owned Heinz claims an 85 per cent share of the £14 million market for baby foods with Gerber another American company holding some 13 per cent. The lion's share of the baby rusk market – some 90 per cent, goes to Ovaltine, owned by the Swiss Sandoz. Britain does better in the cereals and nuts baby foods but both Ovaltine and Gerber maintain a growing share of the market.

Heinz has the largest food factory in this country. Their 57 varieties are familiar trade names and the company has been part of the British way of life since 1917. A subsidiary of H J Heinz of Pittsburgh it employs more than 8,000, its board of directors is predominantly British (three Americans out of a total of 12) and from its authorised capital of £25 million almost £20 million ordinary and £250,000 preference shares are owned by its American parent. Heinz is perhaps best known for its baked beans (the well-known slogan was coined by the British branch of its American advertising agency Young & Rubicam) and it has something like 60 per cent of this £30 million market. Its main competitor is Crosse & Blackwell owned by the Swiss Nestlé. Heinz also maintains a steady 83 per cent of the tinned spaghetti market.

Breakfast cereals are mainly American – Kelloggs claim 57 per cent of the market with brands such as Corn Flakes, Ricicles, Frosties, Sugar Smacks, Coco Pops, All Stars, All-Bran and Rice Krispies. The British owned Weetabix has a 16 per cent share and two American controlled companies – Nabisco and Quaker Oats have a 12 and 11 per cent share respectively with Welgar, Cubs and Shreddies (Nabisco) and the Quaker brand name products. Another popular cereal is Grape Nuts made by the former Alfred Bird, now a subsidiary of General Foods of New York.

Processed cheese shows Kraft (a fully-owned subsidiary of National Dairy Products Corporation) and Swift (also an American owned subsidiary company) taking some three-quarters of the market between them. When it comes to manufactured cheese Kraft has some 70 per cent of the market with Unigate; the Anglo-Dutch Unilever product Milkana and Nestlé (Swiss Knight) bringing up the rear.

The most popular foreign cheeses on sale in this country are the Dutch Edam and Gouda whose total sales amount to approximately 7,200 tons per year; Danish Blue (3,000 tons annually) the French Camembert and Brie together accounting for over 1,000 tons a year; the Italian Gorgonzola slightly more at 1,100 tons a year; the Swiss Emmentaler (large holes) and Gruyere (smaller holes and not to be confused with Emmentaler) at almost 400 tons a year and the French St Paulin and Port Salut at 500 tons per year. These cheeses are imported into the UK and not manufactured here.

Cooking fats shows the Anglo-Dutch Unilever subsidiary Van den Bergh taking 67 per cent of total sales with Stork, Blue Band, Echo, Summer County and the Kosher Tomor. The only other brand with more than five per cent of the market is Kraft. Van den Bergh with Cookeen, Spry and White Cap has just as strong a hold on the cooking fat market. Brown & Polson's Mazola has a third of the total sales of vegetable oils. This company is a wholly owned subsidiary of Corn Products of New York. Kraft is its nearest competitor in this market. Heinz again dominates the olive oil market; salad creams are also Heinz territory (80 per cent) and Crosse & Blackwell (15 per cent), Kraft having a small share of the remainder of the market.

Salada Foods of Canada has moved into the British market and set up a subsidiary. The company produces a wide range of foods and already controls Askeys Wafers.

The major part of the canned fish market is held by another Unilever subsidiary John West, and Unilever also owns the Mac Fisheries chain of shops. In canned meats the American Libby; Armour (a subsidiary of International Packers); the Unilever-owned Unox; the Dutch Ye Olde Oak and Danish Plumrose do not leave a great deal of any sector of the market to the locals, other than corned beef. Here the British Fray Bentos takes the major share with the American Libby coming in second. The Chicago-based Swift is one of the largest meat importers/distributors in this country with more than 80 branches. Walls, the Unilever subsidiary is the market leader in sausages. Oppenheimer Casing, a large manufacturer of sausage skins, has a Chicago parent company. Franco a subsidiary of the Pittsburgh company of the same name makes sausage-linking machines.

The Boston food firm William Underwood recently acquired a 26 per cent equity in Shippam. For its interest Underwood passed over the business of J H Senior whose main lines are steak and kidney pies and fruit puddings. Seniors was bought by Underwoods from Nurdin & Peacock in 1967. Under the terms of the deal Shippams also have the sole UK manufacturing and marketing rights for Underwood products which include Devilled Ham (a US brand leader), Chicken Maryland and Boston Beans. The main producers of sauces are Heinz with its 50 per cent hold on tomato ketchup, and Crosse & Blackwell. The best known brands of brown sauces are the British HP; Daddies and OK, two more British companies and Lee & Perrins which is 60 per cent owned by an American parent of the same name. Marela Pickles is a subsidiary of the American concern W R Grace; Crosse & Blackwell is again a brand leader in pickles and vinegar. Escoffier sauces and flavourings is an American owned subsidiary, the parent company being Heublen.

Unilever through its Birds Eye subsidiary holds the frozen food market with a 65 per cent share. Other well-known Unilever brand names are Surprise (dehydrated vegetables), Smethurst, Vesta and Tempo.

At the end of 1967 Findus and Fropax merged their UK frozen food interests; under the terms of the deal the Swiss Nestlé (which owns Findus) acquired 21 per cent of the equity of Fropax, the shares of which were jointly owned by Lyons and Union International. The net result is that the three leading brand names – Findus, Eskimo, Frood are now owned by Nestlé (50 per cent of the voting equity), Union International and Lyons having the remainder. Fropax and Glacier Foods jointly own an ice cream and frozen food distribution system. Nestlé has also acquired some three-quarters of the 21 per cent holding of the voting equity of Glacier Foods, so that the Findus/Fropax merger gives the group some 20 per cent of the UK market for frozen foods. Kraft recently entered the frozen food market by buying the British firm Brains.

Unilever continues its hold in the ice cream field with a 37 per cent share through its fully-owned subsidiary Walls. Walls merged with Mr Whippy in 1963 to increase its lead over its main British competitor Lyons, which currently has some 35 per cent of the market.

In desserts Heinz holds 75 per cent of canned sweet puddings (mainly sponges); Crosse & Blackwell has a ten per cent share; for packet pie fillings the two Americans – Royal (owned by Standard Brands) and the General Foods subsidiary Bird's share the market with 75 and 25 per cent respectively. Custard powder is dominated by Bird's (65 per cent of sales), other important manufacturers include Brown & Polson, the Corn Products subsidiary, and the Swiss Maggi. Blancmanges again shows Brown & Polson with a 75 per cent share with Birds active to a smaller extent. H J Green is well-known for custard powders, sponge cake mixtures, table desserts and jellies. This is a fully owned subsidiary of the Pillsbury Co of Minneapolis; it employs 250 at its Hove works and also owns Borwick's the baking powder people. Another National Dairy Products subsidiary is Mitcham Foods which makes jellies and is active in the margarine, fat and processed cheese areas through its link with Kraft.

Canned fruits shows Libby's well in the lead and canned vegetables is another Unilever province through its Batchelor subsidiary.

The brand leader in instant potatoes is the Mars subsidiary Dornay Foods whose products Yeoman and Dine hold some 70 per cent of the market. Cadbury, British owned, is also entering this growing market. Money is currently being invested in plant to produce frozen chips. A £1 million production line, believed to be the largest in Europe is being installed in Scarborough by McCain Foods of Canada, which has operated in Britain since 1965. It holds some 30 per cent of the market currently worth £30 million. A challenger is W B Pellew-Harvey of Reading which, in conjunction with Potato Service of New York, plans to operate a large plant in Lincolnshire early in 1969.

The major supplier of potato crisps is British Golden Wonder (the Imperial Tobacco subsidiary), Smiths Crisps is the second largest manufacturer (the American General Mills has a ten per cent stake in this company), then follows Crimpy Crisps which is owned by the US group controlling Pepsi-Cola.

Condensed milk is dominated by three American owned companies: Carnation (owned by General Milk Products) which has had its own milk-processing factory at Dumfries since before 1939 and more than 40 per cent of the market; Nestlé's Ideal with about 24 per cent and Libby around ten per cent. In tinned cream, Nestlé has a third of the market. Smith Kline & French's subsidiary Avoset produces a number of toppings, dairy products and soft ice cream mixes.

The majority of the British tinned soup market is held by American owned companies. Heinz has some 60 per cent, Crosse & Blackwell 22 and Campbells, a fully owned subsidiary of the Campbell Soup Co of New Jersey, 16 per cent. In the field of meat and vegetable extracts and stock cubes Brown & Polson's subsidiary Knorr and Crosse & Blackwell's Maggi have only made small inroads on the British owned Oxo and Bovril products. Unilever however has recently entered the dry soup mixes field.

Sun-Maid Raisins are American owned, the parent company being in California. The traditional British jam and marmalade has also come in for some overseas investment. James Keiller the old Dundee firm is a subsidiary of Nestlé (through Crosse & Blackwell); Frank Cooper famous for marmalades, preserves, honey, horse-radish, mint sauce, diabetic products and tinned fruit and vegetables is a fully owned subsidiary of Corn Products and employs some 300 in turning out these goods.

Doughnuts are made by Dunkin Donuts, a British subsidiary of Universal Food Systems of Massachusetts. DCA Industries, whose parent is in New York makes the equipment used for manufacturing doughnuts. They also make cereal mixes, doughnut and cake mixes, batter mixes and the like. A dominant name in cake mixes is Mary Baker, a Nabisco subsidiary. Nabisco (actually an abbreviation of National Biscuit Company) set up in the UK in 1908, employs more than 1,000 and has three American directors on its board of nine. Nabisco is also known for its Ritz crackers and its Frears biscuits.

Lavery, a DCA subsidiary, makes a wide range of cake mixes under the trade name Lamix and is also known for its Harlequin range of Christmas puddings. Betty Crocker, the General Mills subsidiary, pulled out of Britain some years ago but returned last year to renew the challenge.

Corn Products, through Brown & Polson, has an almost monopolistic hold on glucose syrups, dextrose, solid glucose, caramel, brewing sugars and above all starch. It is also an active producer (through its Corn Products (Sales) subsidiary) of animal feedstuffs, gums and crude maize oil.

Fyffes bananas have been imported into the UK since 1901. Elders & Fyffes is owned by American United Fruit of Boston and holds more than 40 per cent of the banana market. The Dutch owned Geest Industries claims about 45 per cent. Another United Fruit subsidiary is George Jackson the wholesale fruit, flower and potato merchants. Fyffes also recently bought the fruit and vegetable wholesalers George Monro.

Heudebert Foods are French owned; Primula crispbread is a Norwegian subsidiary and Beatrice Foods, American controlled by the Chicago company of the same name manufactures and exports all types of ready-to-eat Chinese foods. The Dutch owned British Fermentation Products is a large producer of yeast and bakers sundries; British Arkady is another major producer of baking yeast, soya flour and pre-mixes, its parent being Ward Foods of New York. Swedish Felix make a popular range of tinned foods including vegetables, beetroot and cranberries.

The slimming foods battle has been under way for some time with Unicliffe, one of the American owned Pfizer group active with Limmits and Trimetts. Procter & Gamble whose head office is in Cincinnati is known for a wide range of slimming foods including Crisbak, Sweetex and Selex. Two other popular sugar-substitutes are Hermesetas, made by the Swiss CIBA and Sucron made by the US owned Ashe Laboratories. High-protein, low-starch loaves sell to the tune of some £20 million a year. The brand leader is Slimcea in the Cavenham Foods group. Cavenham Foods is 51 per cent French owned by one of Source Perrier's subsidiaries and in turn, Cavenham owns 50 per cent of UFICO, the Perrier combine. Other Cavenham products are Procea and Nutrex. A new slimming pill recently introduced is Ayds from Cuticura the soap people, a subsidiary of the American Purex group. Ashe also makes a range of slimming pills and the company is active in non-fattening sweets and chocolate preparations.

Animals also share the national preference for foreign invested foods. Petfoods, a Mars subsidiary, has 60 per cent of the dog food market, 20 per cent of canned cat foods and leads in the bird seed stakes. Petfood brands include Kit-e-kat, Whiskas, Minx and Dine (for cats), Lassie, Chappie, Pal, Buster, Frolic and Pedigree Chum (for dogs), Trill Trillet, Spray and Swoop (birds). Quaker Oats recently entered the canned dog food market (Full-o-pep) and John Morrell with a Chicago parent, which also distributes for another American, Stokely-Van Camp is a major supplier of pet foods.

Through its animal feeding stuffs division, including British Oil & Cake Mills and Silcocks, Unilever maintains a strong hold on the cattle, poultry and pig feeds markets. Procter & Gamble is also active in the manufacture of animal feeds.

British owned firms still lead in chocolate and sugar confectionary, Cadbury and Rowntrees taking a 60 per cent slice between them. The American Mars holds five per cent of the market with Mars Bars, Milky Way and Bounty. Mars employs more than 3,000 and has been established in Britain for more than 30 years. Other Mars brand names include Maltesers, Galaxy, Treets, Spangles and Opal Fruits. Nestlé, the Swiss company, markets a number of popular chocolate products. The Dutch owned Bensdorp and five Swiss owned confectionary producers – Van Melle (whose Fruitella and Tellamint do well in local cinemas), Tobler (a Nestlé subsidiary), Tobler Meltis (not to be confused with the Nestlé group), is owned by Chocolat Tobler AG), Lindt and Suchard do well in the higher-price chocolate and confectionary market. The American Wrigley has an almost world monopoly in chewing gum and also popular in cinemas are Life Savers a joint subsidiary of the US Squibb Beech-Nut and the British H S Whiteside.

An effort to break into the UK market for sugar cane molasses, at present dominated by a Tate & Lyle subsidiary, is being made by a new concern, International Molasses which is 70 per cent owned by the National Molasses Company of Pennsylvania. The new company has opened two deep-water terminals at Hull and Liverpool.

Packet tea is still a British stronghold but the teabag market is held by the American controlled Tetleys, another subsidiary of Squibb Beech-Nut, with some 70 per cent.

Instant coffee is very much under overseas influence. The Swiss Nestlé product Nescafe and the American General Food's Maxwell House are the two top selling brands; Standard Brands, another American, markets a ground tinned coffee under the trade name Chase & Sanborn; the British Lyons is, however, dominant in coffee beans and ground coffee. A foreign contender in the cocoa and drinking chocolate stakes is Van Houten, owned by the American W R Grace and for other night-time drinks the Swiss Wander's Ovaltine shares popularity with the British Horlicks. Wander was recently taken over by another Swiss company – Sandoz.

It would be a sad day for Great Britain if it was to yield its beer interests to the invading foreigner, although Canadian Breweries has a four per cent stake in Bass Charrington, Britain's biggest brewing group. Canadian Breweries is famous for its Carlings Lager which is one of a number of imported beers and lagers sold in Britain. The Danish Carlsberg lager is the most popular of the imports and a stronger version of this drink has just been introduced. Carlsberg has three separate selling organisations in this country. Schlitz 'the beer that made Milwaukee famous' is about to appear in the greater London area through Watney Mann outlets. This is one of two agreements between Watney Mann and the Jos Schlitz Brewing Co; under the second Watneys get their own back on the Americans and sell Red Barrel through the Schlitz marketing organisation. German Lowenbrau, 'most expensive beer in the world' is manning a counterattack on the expensive end of this market.

Coates of Plymouth, the gin people, are owned by Schenley Industries of New York. Apollinaris, a leading producer of mineral water is a subsidiary of the German Dortmund Union. Seven-Up – the carbonated soft drink is American, so is Canada Dry along with the ever popular Colas – Pepsi and Coca.

The Unilever soft drink Tree Top has ten per cent of a market which is otherwise predominantly British.

Wines, fortified wines and aperitifs are imported into Britain and so do not come within the scope of this survey, but the Italian Cinzano, the French Dubonnet and the Dutch Erven Lucas Bols all have fully owned subsidiaries in this country.

Schenley Industries has made considerable inroads into the Scotch whisky market. This company now controls Long John Distilleries, D Johnston the Islay blenders, Stanley Holt (also whisky blenders), together with wine and spirit merchants Sherbrand. The House of Seagram (Seager Evans being another fully owned subsidiary of Schenley Industries) produces a number of spirit lines including gin, cream sherry, rum, egg flip and vodka. Seagrams also has 35 per cent of United Vintners the retail subsidiary of International Distillers & Vintners.

John Jameson the whiskey distillers is Irish owned. The Canadian Hiram Walker owns George Ballantine and Inver House Distillers is owned by Publiker International, also American.

The leading manufacturer of metal caps for sealing bottles is Crown Cork & Seal of Philadelphia which owns just on 80 per cent of the British Crown Cork's shares. Crown Cork also has a 25 per cent share of the aerosol market and does not pay royalties or management fees to its parent company.

Hygienic of Bristol is a large manufacturer of drinking straws; Maryland Paper Products has a 50 per cent holding in this company. Barry-Wehmiller, an important manufacturer of bottling machinery has an American parent; British Miller Hydro, active as makers of bottle washing machinery is owned by Miller Hydro of Georgia.

The second largest us tobacco manufacturer, American Tobacco, recently and rapidly stepped up its 13 per cent holdings in Gallaher to 66 per cent and in doing so uncovered a complex network of international marketing operations and brand names rights. Gallaher, which holds some 27 per cent of the British market, makes Cadets, Senior Service, Park Drive, British Benson & Hedges and Kensitas cigarettes together with Hamlet, Manikin, Senator and John Cotton cigars. Gallaher has also just bought the Sobranie trade marks. But British American Tobacco owns the world trade mark rights for the Senior Service brand name and also controls the Benson & Hedges name in a number of important foreign markets, although Philip Morris sells its own brand of Benson & Hedges in the us. Philip Morris is America's fourth largest tobacco firm. It made an unsuccessful take-over bid for Gallaher prior to the American Tobacco move and has the Players Navy Cut rights in the us which it acquired from American Tobacco.

The situation is further complicated because Imperial Tobacco has the British import rights of American Tobacco's Pall Mall and Lucky Strike. The Ogden branch of Imperial Tobacco, formerly owned by American Tobacco, sells Old Gold tobacco flake (an AT brand name) on a long-standing agreement. To add to the confusion American Tobacco owns the UK rights to some Imperial Tobacco trade names such as Wills, Capstan, Gold Flake, Woodbines and St Bruno. BATS in turn controls the export rights for all Imperial Tobacco brands not covered by other agreements.

The American Tobacco control of Gallaher leaves Imperial Tobacco with some 66 per cent of the market. The Rembrandt-Rothman group of South Africa has effective control of Carreras (eight per cent of the market) which in turn owns Alfred Dunhill.

Since its bid for Gallaher was thwarted by American Tobacco, Philip Morris has subsequently won control of Godfrey Phillips, the small UK group which operates mainly overseas. Godfrey Phillips makes cigarettes under the Abdulla, De Reszke and Four Square names, its pipe tobacco brands include Boars Head.

Tiparillo, the small cigar, is being produced under licence at Ipswich following an agreement between Churchman's (part of Imperial Tobacco) and the General Cigar Co of America.

Two French-controlled companies – Rizla and Job – are both important manufacturers of cigarette papers.

Currently the American Eastman Kodak holds patents covering all the most commercially acceptable methods of producing cigarette filter tips from acetate tow. Kodak's four United Kingdom licensees for filter tips are Carreras, Rothmans, British-American Tobacco and Cigarette Components. Another company making acetate tow, Ectona Fibres, whose Cumberland factory was due to come into operation at the end of 1968 is 60 per cent owned by Kodak.

Ronson products takes the major share of cigarette lighters, this company is controlled by the Ronson Corporation of New Jersey and also has a strong hold on the supply of lighter fuel.

The world's leading manufacturer of tobacco machinery is Molins Machine Company whose parent is in Virginia. Molins is currently expanding its Northern Ireland works.

As we go to press Unilever is holding merger talks with Allied Breweries, the second largest brewery group in the UK controlling Ind Coope, Friary Meux, Grants of St James's and Showerings. Allied has 10,000 public houses and off-licences.

3
TRACTION AND FUEL

American investment in the British motor car industry represents 40 per cent of turnover per year. The largest single motor car producer in the UK is the British Leyland Motor Holdings combine which has just about 35 per cent of the car market (1967 figures), but the best selling car in the UK is the Ford Cortina (recently superseded by the new Escort model).

Ford, a fully-owned American subsidiary with an American managing director has some 28 per cent of the UK market with their Anglia, Consul, Corsair, Taunus, Zephyr and Zodiac cars and Thames commercial vehicles.

Ford is the second largest car manufacturer in the world, the largest being the American General Motors. GM operates in Britain through its fully-owned subsidiary Vauxhall and has just over 13 per cent of the UK market. Vauxhall is known for its Cresta, Velox, Victor and Viva cars and its range of Bedford commercial vehicles; it also distributes other General Motors' cars including Buick, Cadillac, Chevrolet, Oldsmobile, Pontiac, Opel and Holden.

Rootes has a 12 per cent share of Britain's car market; 45 per cent ordinary and 62 per cent of its A ordinary capital is owned by the American Chrysler Corporation, the world's third largest car manufacturer. The Rootes range of cars includes Humber, Hillman, Sunbeam and Singer together with Dodge, Commer and Karrier commercial vehicles. Chrysler also owns the French Simca.

Production of cars and commercial vehicles in the UK

Manufacturer	Cars	Commercial vehicles
*British Motor Corporation	539,219	107,099
Ford	440,711	93,861
*Leyland	122,944	23,994
Rootes (including Dodge)	181,226	29,212
Vauxhall	196,877	89,296
**Jaguar (including Daimler and Guy)	21,941	2,601
Rover (including Alvis which makes mainly military vehicles)	42,596	31,282

(figures for 1967 provided by the Society of Motor Manufacturers & Traders)
*Now merged   **Also part of BMC/Leyland

Foreign cars are popular in Great Britain but most of the vehicles bought are either direct imports or assembled here from parts manufactured overseas. Citroen, a fully-owned French subsidiary has a Slough plant, the Italian Fiat has a large distribution network, the Japanese Honda and Datsun and the German Mercedes, BMW and Volkswagen all operate through distributors. Volkswagen sells around 30,000 cars in the UK and its distribution process has been streamlined to six outlets allowing large stocks to be held in this country. Also active are the French Renault, Swedish Saab and Volvo and Italy's Alfa Romeo. One wonders how accurate is the prediction of Ford's Simon E Knudson who forecasts that in ten years' time there will only be ten big motor manufacturers in the world.

The two largest car hire and rental firms, Hertz and Avis, are both American owned. Avis is a subsidiary of the International Telegraph and Telephone Corporation and maintains a fleet of some 2,500 vehicles. Hertz recently acquired by the Radio Corporation of America, was incorporated in Delaware in 1923, it now has 13 wholly owned subsidiaries and operates more than 75,000 vehicles throughout the world. Group operations are carried out by Hertz American Express International an associate company in which Hertz owns 51 per cent. Hertz also owns all the stock of Meyer Bros Parking Systems which with its 47 subsidiaries, operates some 200 car parks in the USA, Puerto Rico and Great Britain. Hertz has a number of interests in this country among which are Hertz Rent-a-Car System; Daimler Hire; United Service Transport; Andrews Southern Transport; Trevor Cars and Blue Belle Coaching Services. United Transport is itself the parent of a group of haulage contractors and is active in the hire of commercial vehicles, coaches and the like.

Another US firm of hire operators, Budget Rent-a-Car is working in Britain by offering franchise deals to local operators. The group has 60 branch offices and a fleet of 1,500 cars here.

The BMC-Leyland link gives this group a clear lead in the market for trucks and commercial vehicles; prior to the merger Leyland had some 17 per cent of the market, BMC 11 per cent. Ford maintains almost 25 per cent, Bedford is similarly placed. Dodge/Rootes the Chrysler subsidiary has around 17 per cent of the market. Also active in commercial trailers and semi all-purpose trailers is York Trailer of Corby, an associate of Canada's York Transport Equipment. Another well-known manufacturer in this field is Highway Trailers, a subsidiary of the American Highway Trailer Industries which employs 150 at its Southampton premises.

Mercedes-Benz, the West German car manufacturer, is also one of the largest makers of buses in Europe. It is re-entering the British market after a lapse of 35 years. Its British concessionaire has become the first bus importer to receive the Ministry of Transport's certificate of fitness.

An electronic car, powered by batteries and with an estimated fuel bill of one shilling for 30 miles was recently demonstrated in London. The company manufacturing this vehicle is UK International Rectifier, which supplies the thyristors for the control unit. UK International Rectifier is jointly owned by Thorn Electrical Industries and the US International Rectifier Corporation. Development of this type of consumer vehicle is possible within the next five years.

Farbenfabriken Bayer the large West German chemical concern recently demonstrated a car constructed entirely in plastic with the exception of the engine, transmission and main suspension. Bayer developed the model in conjunction with BMW the large German motor manufacturers. The East German Trabant construction technique for plastics fabrication for the all-plastic car is being developed in Britain by De la Rue's Formica division.

Britain's BSA is the largest motor cycle manufacturer in Europe but its output cannot compare with the Japanese Honda whose machines sell well in the UK. The scooter market is held by two Italians, Lambretta with 75 per cent and Vespa with the remainder. Neither manufactures in this country. Vespa has just entered the British moped market with its Vespino. The Austrian Steyr-Daimler-Puch organisation has established a sales and marketing organisation in Nottingham.

The motor components industry is a complex and diverse one and has been the subject of many confidential marketing reports. In this sector there is a large amount of foreign capital invested with, as would be expected, a strong American influence. Although Automotive Products is the largest manufacturer of engine components in the UK, this British owned company is not entirely free from overseas interests, being licensed by Bendix, Borg-Warner, Purolator and TRW.

Borg-Warner itself is extremely active in the British motor components market, and the UK subsidiary employs 1,700 at its Letchworth plant making automatic transmissions, chains, overdrives and a range of accessories as well as machine tools and chemicals. The American parent is based in Chicago.

The British company Mintex which makes brake and clutch linings also has a licence agreement with Borg-Warner for the outward supply of disc brake pads.

Raybestos-Belaco and H K Porter are two more American interests in the area of brake and clutch linings. SAB Brake Regulator is Swedish owned. Bostrom, the subsidiary of Universal Oil Products of Illinois, makes suspension seating.

Champion Sparking Plug is another American subsidiary whose parent is in Ohio. This company is a brand leader in service units and accessories and has been operating in Britain since 1937. Aircraft-Marine Products a subsidiary of AMP Inc of Pennsylvania makes electronic and electrical components and connectors for the appliance, automotive, aircraft, business machine and many other industries. Four of its six directors are American. Denison-Deri which makes pumps, motors, controls and a number of heavy engineering products is a subsidiary of the American ABEX Corporation. The Ford subsidiary Autolite Motor Products is also active in the sparking plug, wirers, starters and components field.

As we go to press it is announced that Cummins Engine of Indiana, the leading supplier of diesel engines to the US heavy truck market, is to buy out Chrysler Corporation from their joint British venture Chrysler-Cummins in Darlington. This plant has a planned capacity of some 30,000 engines a year.

Ranco Motors, known for control gear and switches, and Stewart-Warner, familiar for a range of components, are both American controlled companies.

Eaton Yale & Towne is yet another large American manufacturer of parts and products for the automotive and allied industries. It has a gear and a transmissions division in the UK and several subsidiaries and also has licensing arrangements with a number of British firms.

Arrow Electric Switches which make manually and magnetically operated switches and motor control gear is a subsidiary of Arrow-Hart & Hegeman Electric of Connecticut.

Höxtersche Gummifädenfabrik Emil Arntz, the German manufacturer of V-belts used in motor vehicles, has decided to build a factory in Londonderry. The company will be known as Arntz Belting.

No-Sag Spring makes a range of motor components including car springs at its Dumbarton factory. Its parent is Lear Siegler of Detroit whose other British subsidiary is TIC Engineers, the communication engineering consultants. The Walker Division of Galt Metal Industries with a Belfast factory is owned by the American Walker Manufacturing and produces car exhaust systems. Cam Gears is a subsidiary of TRW Inc of America, itself owning nine UK subsidiaries in the motor components field including Clifford Motor Components and employing more than 1,300. Trico-Folberth & Schrader's, a division of Scovill Manufacturing of Connecticut, are American controlled accessory manufacturers. Wichita which manufactures clutches and brakes is licensed by the Texas company of the same name.

British Twin Disc, whose parent is Twin Disc Clutch of Wisconsin, manufactures a range of components including clutches, marine gears, reduction axles and drive units. The company also acts as licensee for its parent's products which cover fluid couplings, torque converters and the like.

Among European investments in this country is the French owned Solex which makes carburettors and the German Klockner-Moeller which manufactures electrical control gear, motor starters and ancillary equipment. One of the best known types of car washing equipment found here is Harlesden Superwash; this company is a subsidiary of the American Sherman Car Wash Equipment.

Perkins Engines, a subsidiary of the Canadian Massey-Ferguson, which claims to be the world's largest manufacturer of diesel engines, has just introduced a range of petrol engines. Perkins exports 85 per cent of its output.

International Harvester, the US concern, now markets its own anti-freeze product in Britain.

In the field of ball and roller bearings, the largest company manufacturing in the UK is the Swedish Skefko Ball Bearing. The British company was founded in 1910 three years after it began its Swedish activities. More than one in ten of ball bearings produced are made by SKF, a third of the bearings produced go to the motor industry and a similar number to the electrical trades. Second largest in Britain is the American Fafnir Bearing which has a factory in Northern Ireland, the parent company being located in Connecticut. Also active in the UK in the field of high precision ball bearings is Barden Corporation, a subsidiary of another Connecticut manufacturer.

The British Dunlop has 40 per cent of the tyre market, but it has been estimated that two-fifths of this country's tyres are produced by American controlled manufacturers. Some 45 per cent is shared more or less equally between the two Americans, Firestone and Goodyear and the French owned Michelin. Firestone is building a new factory at Wrexham, and both Michelin and Goodyear are expanding into premises in Northern Ireland. The remainder of the market is split between the British owned Avon and the Italian Pirelli.

Pirelli now specialises in the production of radial tyres, formerly the Michelin province, and is due to open a new £3·5 million factory in Carlisle during 1969 to strengthen its position in the market. Radials now account for 17 per cent of the replacement market and are increasingly being used as standard equipment of new cars. Pirelli's Cinturato tyres are fitted on 70 per cent of the Rover 2000's and on most of the Ford Corsair's 2000E range. Imported tyres, particularly from Czechoslovakia (Semperit) and Japan (Yokohama) are taking a growing share of the replacement market, but to date tyre imports are not much more than one million units.

A Dutch rubber company – Vredestein International which markets one of the largest range of tyres in the world – 600 plus – is currently making a determined effort to enter the UK market. Albany Tyres has been appointed for the London area as the first of a number of regional franchise holders which will distribute the Vredestein products.

Uniroyal is an American controlled company with an active tyre division. This company also makes a range of fabricated rubber products. Two other American subsidiaries, Kelly-Springfield and Seiberling Rubber, both manufacture tyres and rubber products.

Tyre valves are made by Bridgeport Brass at their Lisburn factory. This company is owned by National Distillers & Chemical Corporation of New York. Abex Engineering is a large manufacture of tyre moulds whose parent is also in New York.

Tractors and agricultural equipment is dominated – 60 to 70 per cent of the market – by American/Canadian companies producing or manufacturing to North American specification. Out of a total of the £229 million market for agricultural machinery £72 million was turned over by the five foreign owned manufacturers. Massey-Ferguson, the Canadian controlled company, is the leading tractor manufacturer. Massey-Ferguson's nearest competitor in tractors is Ford; the majority of the remainder of this market is held by the American-owned Caterpillar Tractor which is the world's largest manufacturer of earth moving equipment and building trucks; Euclid, the General Motors subsidiary is also a leading manufacturer of earth moving equipment; International Harvester is another American company which also makes other mechanised farm equipment and crawlers; the American Hyster is similarly active in mechanical handling equipment as is Gravely Tractor, a Studebaker subsidiary. The Italian Fiat has both a tractor subsidiary and a tractor spares distribution centre in this country. Allis-Chalmers, which makes tractors but is better known for combine harvesters, earth moving equipment and pumps is a fully-owned American subisidiary which employs 500 in Britain. Koedel & Boehm, one of Germany's largest manufacturers of agricultural machinery has set up a British marketing offshoot in Norfolk.

Earth moving equipment is dominated by a British company – Hymic which has 40 per cent of sales. The British J C Bamford and Canadian Massey-Ferguson are its nearest competitors. The French company Poclain does not manufacture in Britain but has developed a high-powered marketing network through four distribution centres (a fifth was due to open during 1968) and recently doubled its sales force. Its UK turnover is nearly £1·5 million and the company plans a 60 per cent expansion programme. New Holland, active in combine harvesters, is the UK farm machinery end of the American Sperry Rand. Further information on earth moving equipment will be found in the civil engineering section of this book.

By the end of 1968 £100 million or more will have been spent on petroleum refining projects during the year and the investment for the period 1968-70 is expected to total some £276 million. The United Kingdom has become a major target for overseas oil companies and the new refineries will help to reduce Britain's annual import bill of refined products which reached almost 25 million tons in 1967. Exports, already running at over 12 million tons annually should also benefit from the recent increase of capital expenditure in oil refining projects.

World's largest oil companies		
Company	Country of origin	Oil sales (000 barrels/ day)
Esso	USA	4,647
Shell	Holland/ UK	4,094
Texaco	USA	2,369
Mobil	USA	1,721
Standard Oil of California	USA	1,513
BP	UK	1,502
Gulf	USA	1,329

Shell and British Petroleum which market together through Shell-Mex & BP control 45 per cent of the British petrol market. Shell is part of the Royal Dutch Shell group, one of a triumvirate of Anglo-Dutch concerns (Unilever and Philips being the other two). The foundations of the Royal Dutch/Shell group of companies were laid 60 years ago by the fusion of the interests of the Royal Dutch Petroleum Company and the 'Shell' Transport & Trading Company on a 60/40 basis to hold the merged interests of the parent companies. This principle of shared ownership through holding companies has remained unchanged. The holdings of these two parent companies consists mainly in shares in Shell Petroleum and Bataafse Petroleum (Netherlands), each controlling a number of British and Dutch subsidiaries. In fact today the USA holds as much of the Royal Dutch Shell equity as the Netherlands. Sixty per cent of the Royal Dutch share capital is split equally between the United States and the Netherlands. Switzerland and France come next with 17 and 16 per cent respectively. Only four per cent is held in the United Kingdom which does, however, have the dominant (93 per cent) holding in Shell Transport & Trading. Shell has a new refinery at Teesport with a capacity of six million metric tons per annum. At the end of 1968 Shell-Mex & BP acquired 35 of the Heron Group's petrol stations. Some of these will be leased back to Heron but eventually Shell will replace the Heron brand of petrol with its own makes. Heron will continue to expand its garage interests.

Esso is the world's largest oil company; a fully-owned subsidiary of the Standard Oil Company of New Jersey it takes an estimated 27 per cent of the British market. Esso itself has 15 fully-owned UK subsidiaries and is planning to sell its own range of tyres, batteries and car accessories in 9,000 service stations throughout Britain.

Texaco which now owns Regent Oil has 11 per cent of the British market. Texaco is gradually replacing the Regent Brand name with its own; the company intends to enter the fuel oil and lubricants market and has also announced its intention to extend its network of petrol stations. Many of Texaco's joint exploration and producing activities in the

Eastern hemisphere are managed by the 50 per cent owned American Overseas Petroleum (Amoseas) which is affiliated with the Caltex Group.

Until recently Texaco and Standard Oil of California jointly owned Caltex. As a result of this break-up, Standard Oil of California has acquired the Chevron brand name; Caltex is now jointly owned by Socal and Texaco.

The American owned Mobil Oil has some six per cent of the petrol market. Mobil is doubling the capacity of its Coryton refinery to 6·4 million tons.

Another oil complex is the Lindsey oil refinery which is jointly owned by the Belgian Petrofina and the French state-owned Total. Between them these companies control around five per cent of British petrol sales based on nearly 2,000 retail outlets. Their new refinery on the Humber estuary has a capacity of six million metric tons a year. Petrofina was the first of the post-war petrol invaders and also claims a 12 per cent share of the sale of agricultural fuels. Total is the world's eighth largest oil company with assets of about £500 million. It entered the British market in 1960. In July 1968 a major oil terminal was opened as a joint distribution centre by Mobil, Petrofina, Texaco and Shell-Mex & BP.

Refineries are also under construction in the Humber area for the American owned Continental Oil, another large supplier of petroleum products with an estimated capacity of 4·5 million tons a year. Continental Oil has won its second three-year contract to supply gas diesel oil to the National Coal Board. The contract is worth about £1·5 million. Under further contracts totalling £36,800 awarded by the NCB, Shell-Mex & BP and Petrofina will supply fuel oil, kerosene and vaporising oil over the period 1968-1971.

Gulf Oil has completed its third major refinery in the Milford Haven area with a capacity of three million tons. United Refineries, an associate of the Italian state-owned ENI group, is building a two million ton plant on Canvey Island and Murco Petroleum, whose parent is Murphy Oil of Arkansas is about to start work on an equivalent capacity plant on the Clyde.

Major petroleum suppliers with their approximate number of outlets in size order

Company	Country of origin	Brand name(s)	Number of retail outlets supplied
Shell-Mex & BP	Britain-Holland	Shell BP National benzole Power	17,650

Company	Country of origin	Brand name(s)	Number of retail outlets supplied
Esso Petroleum	America	Esso Cleveland Dart	9,756
Texaco	America	Regent (to be replaced by the Texaco brand name during the next five years)	4,405
Mobil Oil	America	Mobil	1,500 (another 100 due to open during 1968)
Petrofina	Belgium	Fina	1,400
Continental Oil	America	Jet Conoco	785
Signal Oil & Gas	America	VIP	700
Total Oil	France	Total	600
**Burmah Oil	Britain	Lobitos Curfew	540
Murco Petroleum (subsidiary of Murphy Oil Corp)	America	Go EP Olympic	448
Tenneco Oil	America	Golden Globe	270
Gulf Oil	America	Gulf	200
Amoco (owned by Standard Oil of Indiana)	America	Amoco	172
Abco Petroleum (owned by Sinclair Oil)	America	Abco	100
Chevron Oil (owned by Standard Oil of California)	America	Chevron	95
Atlantic Petroleum	America	Atlantic	50

(information supplied by the Petroleum Information Bureau)

**Burmah Oil has investments in British Petroleum (owning 24 per cent of BP's shares) and Shell (about 3 per cent of Shell's shares). Its main subsidiary is Castrol which is a market leader in lubricants. As far as petrol is concerned Burmah's principal outlet is Lobitos which is active in Northern Ireland and the Irish Republic markets. Early in 1968 Burmah acquired

Curfew Petroleum and still trades under the Lobitos and Curfew brand names. Motor spirit, kerosenes, gas oil and heavier fuel oils will increasingly be sold under the Burmah mark; lubricants and speciality products under the Castrol name.

Russia is planning to intensify the cut-price petrol war in this country. At present the Russian cut-price Nafta brand petrol is being sold at a few garages in west London, more outlets being planned. Behind these moves is renewed activity by NAFTA (GB) Ltd a £50,000 non-exempt private company set up at the end of 1959 and operating with two Russian directors. Nafta is a resurrection of the ROP brand which claimed ten per cent of the British petrol markets pre 1939. Its shareholders are Russian Oil Products, Anglo-Soviet Shipping Company and Arcos. Russia is also planning to build a refinery of its own in Western Europe.

The Kuwait National Petroleum Company set up an international operation with headquarters in London in 1967. The UK and European markets are currently being investigated with a view to marketing a range of petroleum products. Kuwait National is not to be confused with the Kuwait Oil Company which is a jointed owned subsidiary of British Petroleum and Gulf Oil and is active in petroleum exploration, production and refining.

Other overseas investments in the oil and petroleum industry include American Independent Oil, whose British subsidiary Aminoil acts as a sales office for the parent company; Valvoline, a Division of Ashland Oil & Refinery of New York; Getty Oil whose UK subsidiary Veedol acts as a sales office and Jet-Lube Lubricants with a parent company in California. Lubrizol which manufacturers oil additives is American owned; Lloyds Industries, a Cope Allman subsidiary, has the UK rights for Molyslip oil additives. Two other subsidiaries of American companies are D A Stuart Oil and James B Berry, whose parent is the Quaker State Oil Refining Corp of Pennsylvania.

Britama Tankers is a Gulf Oil subsidiary which also owns eight per cent of Berry Wiggins, the manufacturer of oil refinery equipment and bitumen products.

A number of American interests are represented in the field of petroleum refinery equipment, the major ones being Lummus, whose parent company is Combustion Engineering of Connecticut; Kellogg which is owned by Pullman of Chicago and is also a leading manufacturer of chemical plant; Badger, whose parent company is located in Massachusetts; Petrolite, with a St Louis based parent and Procon of Illinois.

Wayne Tank & Pump is owned by Symington Wayne of New York and this concern is an important manufacturer of petroleum and oil storage equipment. Tokheim, makers of petroleum dispensing equipment, has an Indiana based parent company of the same name.

John Laing, the construction group, has formed a five-year link-up with two French companies for the construction of natural gas and oil pipelines. The company is already associated with the two leading French pipeline contractors, Société Entrepose and Société des Grands Travaux de

Marseille.

Since North Sea oil drilling operations are mainly the province of the oil companies this is an appropriate point to look at overseas investments in this important sphere of operations. There are currently 25 offshore exploration companies and the following indicates their ownership composition:

Group	Country of origin	Percentage ownership
BP Petroleum Development	*UK*	*100*
Burmah North Sea comprising:		
Burmah Oil	*UK*	*40*
Murphy Petroleum	*USA*	*7·5*
Ocean Drilling Exploration	*USA*	*7·5*
A Johnson Exploration	*Sweden*	*5*
Shell/Esso Group comprising:		
Shell Petroleum	*UK/Holland*	*50*
Esso Petroleum	*USA*	*50*
Gas Council/Amoco Group comprising:		
Amoco	*USA*	*30·77*
Amerada	*USA*	*30·77*
Gas Council	*UK*	*23·08*
Texas Eastern	*USA*	*15·38*
American Overseas Petroleum (Amoseas)	*USA*	*100*
Phillips Petroleum Group comprising:		
Phillips Petroleum	*USA*	*35*
Fina Exploration	*Belgium*	*30*
Agip	*Italy*	*15*
Century Power & Light	*UK*	*7·22*
Tarmac	*UK*	*4·26*
Oil Exploration	*a group of private investors formed under the auspices of the Ionian Bank*	*4·26*
Mobil Producing North Sea	*USA*	*100*
Gulf Oil	*USA*	*100*

Group	Country of origin	Percentage ownership
Continental Oil/NCB Group comprising:		
Continental Oil	*USA*	*50*
National Coal Board	*UK*	*50*
Total Oil Marine Group comprising:		
Total Oil	*France*	*30*
Coastal Oil	*France*	*30*
Auxirap	*France*	*30*
Eurafrep	*France*	*4*
Cofrasea Oil	*France*	*3*
Coparex North Sea	*France*	*3*
Arpet Group comprising:		
Arpet Petroleum	*USA*	$33\frac{1}{3}$
British Sun Oil	*UK*	$23\frac{1}{3}$
North Sea Exploitation & Research	*Germany*	*10*
Superior Oil	*USA*	*30*
Canadian Superior	*Canada*	$3\frac{1}{3}$
Signal Oil & Gas Group comprising:		
Signal Oil & Gas	*USA*	*25*
Richfield UK Petroleum	*USA*	*25*
Marathon Petroleum	*USA*	*25*
Cities Service	*USA*	*25*
Place Oil & Gas Comprising:		
Place Oil	*Canada*	*45*
Noranda Mines	*Canada*	*45*
Husky Oil	*Canada*	*10*
Whitehall Petroleum	*UK*	*100*
Placid Oil	*USA*	*100*
Northern & Central Gas	*Canada*	*100*
Allied Chemicals	*Monaco*	*100*

(based on material supplied by the Petroleum Information Bureau)

Marathon Petroleum, subsidiary of the American company, plans to drill for oil in Northern Ireland. Marathon is currently active off the Dutch coast; the Antrim coast petroleum exploration and production licence covers 500 square miles.

The Amex UK North Sea Group and BP have an agreement for joint exploration and exploitation of their respective oil and gas interests. The Amex UK Group comprises:

Amex Petroleum	USA	$33\frac{1}{3}$
Falcon Seaboard Drilling	USA	11
North Sea Selection	UK	$33\frac{1}{3}$
Total Oil Marine	France	11
Coastal Oil and Auxirap	France	11

The Arpet Group has just signed an agreement with the Gas Council for North Sea gas, a Shell-Esso agreement is also thought likely.

Many of the groups drilling for North Sea oil are also exploring both sea and land for natural gas. So far only the Phillips Group has signed a sales contract with the Gas Council.

BP operates with the Gas Council and also holds a licence to operate along the Lancashire coastline with Seaboard of America and Place of Canada and on the east coast with Home Oil of Canada. Continental, Total, Shell-Esso, California-Texaco and Superior, whose parent company is in Houston, all have onshore concessions. Burmah Oil is in partnership with Murphy along the north-east coast. Other groups active in gas drilling operations include Mobil, Gulf, Signal and Placid.

4
COSMETICS AND TOILETRIES

Half the cosmetics consumed in Great Britain are made by American owned concerns, and there is also a high French interest in the perfume field. In the higher price range of cosmetics comes three American owned companies – Helena Rubenstein which was founded in 1908, Elizabeth Arden and Coty a subsidiary of Pfizer and one French concern Lancome (a subsidiary of L'Oreal). The middle price bracket includes a further clutch of American subsidiaries: Revlon, Dorothy Gray (a subsidiary of Lehn & Fink Products), Max Factor, the largest cosmetics and allied products distributor in the UK; Charles of the Ritz and Avon Cosmetics.

Avon runs a direct sales operation and is believed to have picked up 14 per cent or more of the total market in less than nine years of setting up in Britain. The company is currently building a new distribution centre at Corby costing more than £1 million; it has 2,000 people working in Northampton and in its northern distribution centre near Sheffield. In 1959 Avon had only 50 employees in Britain. The direct selling technique is beginning to interest a number of American firms. Shadow Girl, not yet operative over here is trying to enter the market and Pfizer (through its Coty subsidiary) has also expressed interest in this method of marketing. Beauty Counselors has operated in London for sometime using the direct sales approach.

Newly-formed in Britain is another American company – Cosmetic Products (UK) which has been recruiting wholesalers to sell its Don Loper 'hypo-allergenic' cosmetics due to be launched nationally at the beginning of 1969. The operation will work through wholesalers each being assigned a territory of at least 100 retail outlets. The wholesaler is invited to lay down £1,600 worth of stock and is then given several forms of incentives.

Another range of cosmetics which is about to be launched in the UK for those with allergies is the Almay brand, American owned and a market leader in the US, Almay is backed by Aspro-Nicholas, itself Australia founded.

The higher price end of the cosmetic market is being attacked by a Swiss company, Bea Kasser, which claims to be the largest manufacturer of cosmetics in Europe, with sales exceeding £1 million a year. Smith & Nephew currently imports the Juvena range, another top-selling Swiss brand.

The economy brands are led by the American Chesebrough-Pond's with the Ponds and Angel Face range (the company also manufactures under the brand name Vaseline). Chesebrough-Pond's is a public company and is ranked in the USA at number 416 by *Fortune*. The main all-British manufacturer of lower priced cosmetics is Rimmel.

Other American owned general cosmetics manufacturers not holding quite such dominance in the market but nevertheless selling well are Rayette-Faberge; Romney (another Pfizer subsidiary); Siris (which also makes luggage); Tokalon and International Chemical, a subsidiary of American Home Products Corporation and known for its Anne French range.

Unilever cosmetics include Astral, Skinfare, Icilma, Skin Deep, Vinolia and Evette. Currently the company is forming a subsidiary called Pinoya to market the Dura-Gloss range from Arthur Winarick of New York. The range covers over 150 items and eventually Unilever plans to manufacture these cosmetics in Britain under licence to the US manufacturer. Lanolin is made by Hazel Bishop whose parent is in New Jersey. Procter & Gamble is also about to enter the market with a face cream – Cheek to Cheek. Another newcomer to Britain is Ravenhurst Enterprises with a lubricating body cream.

The market for face powder shows a distinct preference for Max Factor (about 40 per cent) with Coty (seven per cent), Ponds, Avon, Rubenstein and Revlon (six per cent each). The only all-British contender of any size is Yardley. Lipsticks follow a similar pattern with Factor leading at 21 per cent, Chesebrough-Pond's having about 15 per cent; Revlon, Avon and Coty share some six to seven per cent each. Yardley has a 14 per cent market share and another British company, Myram Picker has a 12 per cent hold with Gala, Miners and Outdoor Girl.

Eye make-up again puts Max Factor in the lead with Avon, Ponds, Revlon and Helena Rubenstein well placed. A new entrant is Maybelline, distributed by Richards & Appleby, which does well in America. Cutex, a Cheseborough-Pond product, has almost half the market for nail varnish. Sun-tan lotion shows Coty in a strong position.

The only major British producer of perfumes, toilet waters and colognes is Yardley, part of the British American Tobacco group. The French perfume houses have a high proportion of the market and Chanel no 5 is said to be the world's best selling perfume. Avon has some 25 per cent of the perfume market (including toilet water and cologne), Yardley has nine per cent, Coty eight per cent and Max Factor seven per cent. Guerlain, Molyneux, Dubarry, Revillon-Millot, Lucien Lelong and Bourjois are all French owned perfume houses. The US De Witt International recently acquired Potter & Moore, an Albright & Wilson subsidiary.

The old French perfume company Houbigant, now based in the USA has just bought a controlling interest in Abbey Parfumerie, the London concern which has acted as Houbigant's distributor. In the 1930's Houbigant claimed a large share of the British market.

A H Robins, Virginia based with an active British subsidiary, bought Caron perfume in the early part of 1967. Also popular in the perfume and toilet water field are the Unilever products California Poppy and Atkinsons.

Hair colourants are dominated by five major manufacturers all of which are foreign owned. Top of the list is Richard Hudnut, whose parent is Warner-Lambert of New Jersey, claiming some 16 per cent of the market, followed by the French L'Oreal which operates in Britain through its licensee Golden. Other L'Oreal products include bubble bath preparations and after-shave lotion. Elida, the Unilever subsidiary which manufactures Sea Witch, Harmony and Melody claims a 14 per cent market share, about the same percentage as L'Oreal. The other major manufacturers of hair colourants are Toni, the Gillette subsidiary and Clairol, owned by Bristol-Myers. Clairol's two brands are Loving Care and Nice 'n Easy. Bristol-Myers is also well known as the manufacturer of Vitalis and Score. Helene Curtis, the Los Angeles company said to be the world's largest hair products empire has launched a new range of hair beauty products in Britain. The company manufactures in 34 countries.

The familiar hair product Vitapointe is French, with Fulford as its British licensee. Unilever has a good hold on the shampoo market with Sunsilk, Clinic, together with the hair oil Nutrilene. Popular manufacturers of hair sprays include the German Wella, Schwarzkopf, another German concern whose UK subsidiary is Corionol, and the Revlon subsidiary Realistic.

Procter & Gamble is doing well with an initial launch of Head and Shoulders, a medicated shampoo. It is reputed to be aiming at a 25 per cent share of the British shampoo market. Colgate-Palmolive's Goddess Shampoo was recently launched on the UK market.

The value of the toilet soap market is about £22·8 million with Unilever's Lux and Colgate-Palmolive's Palmolive accounting for some 30 per cent. Gillette is entering this sector with a product called Happy Face to be sold through its Toni division.

Quickies, the face cleanser pads, are made by Associated Products whose headquarters are in New York.

Gibbs, a Unilever subsidiary, has between 35 and 40 per cent of the £20 million toothpaste market. Its major brands are SR (17 per cent), Signal (13 per cent), Gibbs Fluoride, Pepsodent, Mentasol and Dentifrice.

Colgate-Palmolive's brands take some 30 per cent of the market. Their Colgate is the most popular make (27 per cent), the company also markets Dental Cream, Fluoride and Ultrabrite. The major British contender, Beecham's Macleans, has about a fifth of the total market. Other well-known brands of American origin include Parke, Davis's Euthymol; International Chemical's Kolynos; Procter & Gamble's Gleam; Stafford-Miller's Amm-I-Dent (the parent company is Block Drug of New Jersey); Bristol-Myers' Ipana and Phillips, Scott & Turner's Phillips.

Halex toothbrushes and hair combs are well known. Halex is a division of Bakelite Xylonite which is jointly owned by the British Distillers and the American Union Carbide.

Electric toothbrushes shows Ronson a clear leader in the British market. Ronson's parent company is in New Jersey.

In deodorants Bristol-Myers' Mum is the outright leader with 19 per cent of this £3 million plus market. Next comes Body Mist, the Beecham product with 16 per cent, American Avon has 13 per cent, and Colgate-Palmolive's Odo-Ro-No claims seven per cent. Factor, Revlon and Gillette are also active. Procter & Gamble is attacking this sector of the market with its deodorant Tempo. Carter-Wallace, the New York manufacturer of pharmaceuticals and cosmetics has a British subsidiary, Cartaret Products in Folkestone. Cartaret manufactures the Arrid range of deodorants and Nair depilatories.

Talcum and baby powders account for £4 million annually. The most popular brand is Avon with 24 per cent, then comes the British owned Yardleys and the American companies Johnson & Johnson and Max Factor each with six per cent; Pond's and Arden each claim two per cent.

Men's toiletries is a growing market currently worth about £9 million. Almost half of this is held by the American Shulton, the world's largest manufacturer of these products, with Old Spice, York Town and Desert Flower. Their board of directors shows two Americans to one British. The company employs about 230 in the UK and recently opened a new plant in Northumberland. Two more American companies, Max Factor and Mennen have five per cent each.

In men's deodorants, Gillette's Right Guard is the best selling aerosol product. This company recently entered the men's hairdressing market with Drive, an aerosol dressing and its Foamy is the most popular brand of aerosol shaving cream. Gillette is also launching a 'hot' aerosol shaving cream. The company claims that six per cent of wet shavers use an aerosol at present but that this is a fast growing sector of the market. Shaving preparations are also the province of the Unilever subsidiary Gibbs (Gibbs' Easy and Erasmic), and the American Colgate-Palmolive; Ingram's shaving cream is made by Bristol-Myers.

The razor blade market is held almost equally by two companies: the American Gillette and the British Wilkinson. Gillette ranks about 200 in the *Fortune* list of leading companies. It acquired the British Auto-Strop Safety Razor Co in 1930, produces 93 per cent of all the safety razors made in this country and is responsible for 76 per cent of razor blade exports.

Other overseas interests in razor blades are Ever-Ready, a subsidiary of Philip Morris which makes Pal and Personna; Schick whose parent company is in Pennsylvania; and Satinex, which has Swedish capital invested in it.

Electric shavers again show strong foreign investments. The Anglo-Dutch Philips is the largest manufacturer followed by two Americans, Ronson and Remington. Remington, a division of Sperry Rand, is moving the European headquarters of its shaver division to London from Connecticut. Schick Electric of Pennsylvania and Sunbeam of Chicago are both active in this sector of the British market. The shavers made by the German Braun, which sell well in Europe, would be better known in the UK were it not for a licensing agreement with Ronson which keeps Braun's shavers out of both Britain and the USA.

The current market for toilet tissue is nearly £25 million. The two manufacturers which dominate the British market are Bowater-Scott and Kimberly-Clark. Bowater-Scott, a joint Anglo-American venture between Bowater UK and the Scott Paper Corporation of America, is currently constructing a new mill at Barrow. Bowater-Scott's Andrex claims 25 per cent of the market. Kimberly-Clark's Delsey has 11 per cent. This company is American but the British Reed Paper Group has a one-third share in its British operations. Kimberly-Clark's Kotex and the American owned Tampax both take a dominant share in sanitary protection applications.

The market for self-adhesive first aid dressings is held by the British Smith & Nephew with Elastoplast having 60 per cent or more and the American owned Johnson & Johnson's Band-aid which takes around 30 per cent. Smith & Nephew recently turned down a take-over bid from Unilever.

Facial tissues constitute a market worth at least £10 million. Kimberly-Clark's Kleenex takes 60 per cent, Bowater-Scott's Scotties has 20 per cent and Satinex, which is partly owned by the Swedish paper company Mo och Domsjö, claims ten per cent. Satinex is currently expanding its North Wales works.

In kitchen papers the major producers are again Bowater-Scott whose Scot-towels claim half this growing market. Kleenex has more than 46 per cent and Satinex, just breaking in, aims at an eventual five per cent share.

5
PUBLISHING, PRINTING AND
ALLIED INTERESTS

Bernard Geis, American publisher of *Valley of Dolls* and similar titillating titles, has just opened a British subsidiary. Overseas interests in the British book world are strong. Father of them all is the Encylopaedia Britannica, almost as old as the United States itself, being founded in 1768. Of its seven directors four are American. Sales of the Britannica and its associated volumes are usually made direct. Phaidon Press noted for its fine art volumes is a subsidiary of Encyclopaedia Britannica.

Corgi Books, one of the biggest paperback publishers in Britain is currently being taken over by an American film, theatre and television company as part of a $49 million deal which provides for National General Corporation of Los Angeles to acquire Grosset & Dunlap, the American firm which owns Bantam Books in the United States and controls Corgi in Britain through another subsidiary, Transworld Publishers. Corgi is the third largest paperback group in Britain with about 20 per cent of the market. Penguin is the largest group with about 40 per cent and the American publisher McGraw-Hill owns ten per cent of Penguin. The other giant in this field is Pan which has a 25 per cent market share.

Doubleday is an old established firm of US publishers among whose interests in this country are Aldus and Rathbone Books. Doubleday is also involved in a partnership with W H Smith entitled Book Club Associates which includes the Literary Guild (whose members are able to select, at time of publication titles at 25 per cent below the net price), the Cookery Book Club and the World Books Club. The Book of the Month Club, whose chairman is Robert Maxwell, has tied up with Diners'

Club in a merchandising drive. Other popular American makes of paper-backs are Ace and Four Square, both subsidiaries of Times-Mirror of Los Angeles, as is the New English Library. Golden Pleasure Books is another paperback range associated with an American concern, Western Publishing of Wisconsin.

Textbook and general publishers are also well represented in Britain. Collier-MacMillan is owned by Cromwell Collier & MacMillan Inc with the British MacMillan. Bowker Publishing; Holt, Rinehart & Winston; Academic Press; John Wiley; Harper & Row and TFH are all American owned. The Grolier Society is another American subsidiary, so is D Van Nostrand. European interests are also well represented. Elsevier Publishing is a subsidiary of the Dutch concern of the same name. Currently Elsevier is making a bid for Misset, another Dutch publisher. If the bid goes through Elsevier will transfer 40 per cent of the Misset shares acquired to Iliffe NTP Overseas, a subsidiary of the International Publishing Corporation with which Elsevier already co-operates.

Recently announced take-overs include Studio Vista by Cromwell-Collier & MacMillan which is also currently making an offer for Cleaver-Hume and Weidenfeld & Nicholson which has sold a 39 per cent holding to Encyclopaedia Britannica.

Bottin International is French; Publication Inter-Europe is owned by Jaeger of Germany. Arnoldo Mondadori Editore, the giant Italian print-ing and publishing company also has an office in London which it opened recently. Mondadori had a turnover of some £40 million in 1967.

The Canadian Geo Publications also has an associate in this country. On the educational side, the American International Correspondence Schools has a British subsidiary known as Intertext. Other American publishers in the UK are Hafner Publishing, King Features Syndicate (owned by the Hearst Corporation), Pall Mall Press (owned by Frederick A Praeger), Quigley Publications, W B Saunders, and Blaisdell Pub-lishing, a subsidiary of Ginn.

Magazine publishers are equally numerous. Largest is the American Reader's Digest Association, which is also active in books and gramophone records. Two of their board of directors are American and they employ 600. *Reader's Digest* has an arrangement with the Automobile Association whereby the former publishes a magazine *Drive* along the lines of its own journal, for AA members. The National Magazine Company, publishers of *Good Housekeeping*, *Vanity Fair*, *Harpers Bazaar* and many other titles is a subsidiary of the Hearst Corporation of New York. The group employs 400 and has been established since 1910.

Condé Nast is part of the American Newhouse printing group, it is famous for *Vogue* magazine, *House and garden* and a quantity of pattern books. Time-Life International has a smart office in Bond Street and employs more than 100 in this country. *Time* magazine itself is printed in Paris and published from its Amsterdam office.

Two technical journal publishers of size are the American McGraw-Hill and the Canadian owned Maclean-Hunter which has a number of subsidiaries and a lengthy list of journals including *British rate and data; Business systems and equipment; Packaging news; Ports and terminals.*

The New Yorker has a London office.

In the music publishing field Gate Music is American owned. Music Corporation of America owns Leeds Music, the London music publishing company. Koppelman-Rubin, the new music publishing subsidiary of Commonwealth United Corporation is reconnoitring the British market prior to opening an office.

The three major publishers of dressmaking patterns are all American – Simplicity, Butterick and McCall.

Hachette, the bookshop, is a subsidiary of the French Librairie Hachette as is Continental Publishers & Distributors which is responsible for distributing the wide range of Hachette publications. Joshua B Powers the publishing representatives are American owned; Albert Milhado which also represents the advertising interests of a wide range of journals is Dutch in origin. The London-based publishers' representatives H P Hart and the New York special projects publishers Benjamin Company have formed a joint concern to pioneer British and European development of the use of books as marketing and sales incentives. The new company, Hart & Benjamin, has its office in Grosvenor Street, London W1.

The press cutting agency Newsclip/Apcut is a subsidiary of Midwest Newsclip of Chicago.

American inroads into greeting cards have been making themselves felt. Hallmark and Rust Craft are both US subsidiaries. Dennisons's which makes gift wrappings, crepe paper, tags and labels has a Massachusetts-based parent. Kaye-Gibson is owned by CIT.

Early in 1968 it was announced that the Official Index to the *Times* newspaper was to be reprinted by Kraus Reprint of Liechtenstein. Many British publishers have their books printed overseas, particularly in Holland. The new Pergamon world atlas was printed in Poland. Two foreign investments in the British printing industry are the Dutch van Boekhoven and Rocappi, the American firm of computer typesetters, part of whose shares are owned by the British Printing Corporation. Bradbury Wilkinson, engravers and security printers, exchanges know-how with the American Bank Note Company.

In the field of printing machinery, British Linotype is a wholly owned American subsidiary which has operated in the UK since 1890 and has anything between 50 and 90 per cent of the market for its various machines. Its main competitor for linotype setting machines is Harris-Intertype another American owned company. Sheridan Machinery also a subsidiary of Harris-Intertype makes magazine binding and string tying machines for the printing industry. This company is licensed by B H Bunn of Chicago. American firms have a major hold on the market for new newspaper production techniques such as computer typesetting and photographic setting – British Linotype also owns K F Paul which has developed a photocomposing machine of considerable potential. Pulp and paper machinery suppliers include the Swedish controlled Boving and the

American owned Black-Clawson which has 1,500 employees. Peter Dixon the paper makers is spending £2 million on expansion, a proportion of which is on the installation of a new papermaking machinery at its Grimsby plant. These are being built by Black-Clawson International and included in the installation is Black-Clawson's Verti-Forma, the first time this is being used in Britain. The technique was developed in the US and with its use it is claimed that the machine is capable of making paper at speeds in excess of 3,000 per minute. These machines are being made at Black-Clawson's plant in Newport. Paper machines and allied equipment is manufactured by Beloit-Warmsley International of Kingston whose parent is the Wisconsin-based Beloit Corp.

Another company active in printing and processing equipment for photographic, x-ray and graphic arts fields is Pako of Southampton, whose parent company is in Minneapolis. Three more large American owned manufacturers of printing and bookbinding machines are Miehle-Goss-Dexter, Ludlow Typograph and Smyth-Horne. Fishburn Printing Ink is owned by Interchemical Corporation of New York.

Star Paper Mills of Blackburn, which produces coated printing papers is 90 per cent owned by Kymmene of Finland. Eckman of Sweden has two sales agents in Britain, Acorn Papers of London and White's Swedish Paper Sales in Glasgow. Domtar is Canadian owned. St Regis Paper of New York has two subsidiaries in the UK, one bearing the same name as the parent company, the other being Amalgamated Packaging Industries. Associated Paper Mills has an agreement with Knowlton Bros, another US concern, to manufacture certain of each other's specialist papers. Some 25,000 fully paid ordinary shares have been issued to Knowlton with an option on a further 25,000. Knowlton has subscribed for a further 84,000 shares at 8s 6d per share to cover the costs of plant alterations and additions at Associated Paper Mills works. The capital of APM is £3 million.

The plastics industry has come up with a new development which challenges the traditional supply of coated paper for quality printing. A plastic printing sheet which looks and feels like paper has been made by BXL, part of the Bakelite-Xylonite group owned by Distillers and Union Carbide. Called Polyart, the new material is almost impossible to tear.

Ernest Scott, manufacturers of paper pulping machinery, is owned by Ritter Pfaudler of New York.

The paper converting division of Oxley Industries is negotiating an association with an American company with a view to manufacturing paper in the UK. Oxley is currently expanding its Bolton factory.

6
TEXTILES, CLOTHING AND FOOTWEAR

In 1904 Samuel Courtauld bought the exclusive rights to manufacture and sell viscose in the United Kingdom from the Viscose Spinning Syndicate for £25,000. Today through a vast complication of international technical and commercial agreements relating to cellulosic fibres, Courtaulds is the dominant supplier of viscose and acetate cellulose fibres and the company has extensive participation in the textile industry. Britain's ICI is responsible for around 60 per cent of the synthetic fibres of which nylon is the best known.

Monsanto Textiles (until recently it was known as Chemstrand) has about a one-third share of the current capacity for acrylic fibres in Britain and some ten per cent of the nylon capacity. Monsanto is the largest all-purpose American chemical concern in the UK. It is fully-owned by the Monsanto Corporation of St Louis and produces Blue C nylon-66 and nylon filament yarns at its Dundonald factory. A Monsanto subsidiary, Lansil, produces filament acetate yarn at its Lancaster plant and has some 15 to 20 per cent of the acetate yarn capacity in Britain. The company is about to build an acrylonitrile plant probably in the Tees-side area, acrylonitrile is the raw material from which Courtelle, Orlon and Acrilan are derived. The acrylics come closest of the synthetic materials to the properties of wool and are in growing demand for carpets, knitwear and in blends with other fibres. Currently Monsanto imports the acrylonitrile it needs for the production of its Acrilan at its plant in Northern Ireland.

The only UK producer of acrylonitrile is Border Chemicals, a company owned two-thirds by British Petroleum and one-third by Imperial Chemical Industries. Border's main customer is Courtauld's which produces acrylic fibre under the brand name of Courtelle.

The other important acrylic fibres used in the UK market are Du Pont's Orlon and Lycra which the company at present imports from Europe but which will soon be made in Northern Ireland. Du Pont is a fully-owned subsidiary of the American E I Du Pont de Nemours; Lycra has a near monopoly (estimated 95 per cent) of the elastomeric yarn trade; Orlon taking about a fifth of the acrylic fibre market. Dacron is another Du Pont fibre similar to Terylene.

Du Pont's latest man-made fibre due to be put on the market in early 1969 is called Qiana whose development is planned to extend into the UK probably by way of licensees. Already the fibre boasts good absorbability and easy-care qualities together with an ability to hold colours and resist fading.

An important polyester fibre is Trevira which is made by the German company Farbwerke Hoechst. At present, these fabrics are being produced in the UK from imported yarn but Hoechst, Europe's biggest polyester producer, has under construction a polyester fibre plant in Limavady whose initial capacity is to be ten million lb a year. This plant is due to open in 1970. Trevira presents a challenge to ICI's Terylene and its tex-turised version, Crimplene, which until recently enjoyed a monopoly position in the market for polyester fibres. Since Terylene's patent protec-tion has run out in most respects, British Enkalon, a subsidiary of the Dutch AKU group, last year began production of its own Terlenka polyester also in Northern Ireland. Total UK Terylene capacity is said to be almost 200 million lb a year. The new Trevira plant will produce a proportion of its output as filament yarns suitable for texturising. ICI has concentrated almost exclusively on the double-jersey market for Crimplene, but Hoechst has developed variations suitable for warp-knitting and weaving offering the opportunity to broaden the markets for textured polyester.

Patchogue-Plymouth, an offshoot of the Standard Oil Company of Indiana, is to open a large plant at Consett for the manufacture of woven polypropylene fabrics. The main outlet for these fabrics is in primary backings for tufted carpets. The UK operation will be a division of Amoco, another subsidiary of Standard Oil of Indiana.

Other well-known overseas man-made fibres in use in the UK are Diolen (German), Leacril (Italian), Grilon (Swiss) and the Japanese Amilan.

Lurex manufactures a large share of the metallic yarn output from its Windsor factory and is associated with Dow Chemical of Michigan.

Marglass is one of the leading producers of glass fibre, another material which is being used increasingly in furnishings and certain light construct-ion work. It is jointly owned by Courtaulds and the American concern United Merchants & Manufacturers through the latter's subsidiary, Spun Glass. Riverdale, also owned by United Merchants, imports the Uniglass range of glass fibre curtain fabrics. Two other United Merchants subsi-diaries are Tate and British Silk Dyeing. Tate, merchant converters of Leeds, are prominent in the rayon blend trousering trade and British Silk

Dyeing of Balloch are commission fabric dyers and finishers.

Borg Fabrics of Whitstable is a subsidiary of the American Amphenol Corporation and is a leading manufacturer of silver-knit and deep pile fabrics including the simulation furs and fleece materials which are rapidly gaining popularity both with the clothing trade and the consumer. Borg employs more than 250 and three of its four directors are American. Another American owned company, Glenoit, is an active manufacturer of simulation fabrics.

Ames Textile Corporation of Massachusetts has two British subsidiaries – Ames Mills which makes industrial knitted fabrics and Balleymoney Manufacturing, as yet fairly small but expecting to grow in size, which manufactures carded cotton yarns.

At the beginning of 1968 Viyella had to sell its 50 per cent stake holding in the profitable Bondina (BDA) manufacturer of non-woven fabrics so that it (Viyella) could enter the non-woven fabric manufacturing business on its own account. The purchaser was Viyella's partner in Bondina, Pellon Corporation of Massachusetts, itself a wholly owned affiliate of the West German group Freudenberg KG.

On the licensing side, the International Wool Secretariat announced at the beginning of April 1968 that it had signed an official agreement with the USSR to exchange manufacturing rights and licences on new technological processes and products using wool.

Lastex Yarn & Lactron Thread is associated with Uniroyal. Doverstrand, which manufactures synthetic latex, is jointly owned by International Playtex of America and Revertex of London. Lana-Knit, the jersey fabrics manufacturer is a subsidiary of Jonathan Logan. Waterside Mill of Bury, weavers of industrial fabrics, is now owned by Deering Milliken of New York which also has a London subsidiary of the same name. Grahams (Seacroft) is owned by Schlegel Manufacturing of New York. This company specialises in narrow fabrics. J P Stevens, again with a New York parent company, manufactures glass fibre decorated fabrics. Tuck Tape is a subsidiary of the Canadian Dominion Tape; Ulster Textile Mill, makers of spun cotton yarn, is a subsidiary of T J Stevenson of New York.

A number of European textile houses have sales offices and distributors in Britain including Bischoff, Taco, Schwarzenbach, Descours Genthon and Zurra from Switzerland; Blin & Blin of France; Montana of Austria and Mölnlycka and Hettemarks of Sweden. Schappe, the Swiss company active in acrylic yarns and polyester fibres, manufactures in the UK as does Stünzi Silks and Winterthur Silks, two more Swiss-based concerns.

Recently introduced into the British market is a Dutch carpet tile, Heugafelt, manufactured by Van Heugten of Amersfoort. Sales now run at over £1 million a year and the company and its agents are stepping up their promotional activities. Roberts Consolidated Industries, a US company, has introduced a carpet-fixing device.

Barwick Mills is owned by E T Barwick of Georgia which claims to be the world's largest tufted carpet makers. Barwick Mills started its UK operations in 1966 manufacturing the first polyester carpet to be made in

Britain. In the field of household textiles David Moseley of Manchester, an Avon Rubber subsidiary, has signed an agreement with the New Jersey firm Raybestos-Manhattan for the manufacture and marketing of Clupak blankets. Sleepeezee, the bedding concern, is a member of the American-Canadian Simmons Group.

A leading blanket manufacturer is Lantor which is a jointly owned subsidiary of English Sewing and West Point-Pepperell of Georgia. Two other blanket manufacturers of size – Charles Early & Marriott and Wormalds – are licensees for American manufacturing processes.

Leesona which has a Rhode Island parent is a leading manufacturer of textile machines. Courtaulds has the sole UK rights for Czech water jet looms and also uses the Swiss Sulzer double width looms in its Carlisle factory. Wilson, Longbottom & Lansco which makes looms and allied machinery is jointly owned by Lansdowne Steel & Iron of Pennsylvania and Wilson & Longbottom of Barnsley. Singer-Cobble Bros, manufacturers of carpet tufting machinery, is a division of Singer of Tennessee. Dayco Rubber, the American-owned company, makes rubber and synthetic accessories for the textile trade at its Dundee works. The Belfast manufacturer of textile colours, Tennants Textile Colours, has a minority interest held by Interchemical Corporation of New York.

Simon Ackerman, well-known in the clothing and footwear trades, is American owned. The Manhattan Shirt Company maintains a sales office in London but Cluett Peabody's Arrow shirts are no longer produced in the UK. The major supplier of sportswear and swimsuits is Jantzen which is licensed by the Oregon company of the same name. A major attack on the market for women's woollen coats, dresses and skirts is planned by Sunbeam, Ireland's major textile group, which is installing a commercial production line incorporating new German combined weaving-knitting looms.

The French Christian Dior has a retail shop and a marketing operation in this country. Pierre Cardin operates mainly through licensees, his cloak and suit line being produced by a Great Universal Company subsidiary. The French Damart is well known for cellular underwear for men and also for blankets. This company has a factory in Yorkshire. Kattenburgs, makers of waterproofs and raincoats under the trade name Kattex, is Dutch owned. Walter Whitaker also known for weatherproofs is associated with Junex of Sweden.

In footwear, Joyce is American owned as is Baby Deer whose parent is Trimfoot of Missouri. Hush Puppies, a shoe which originated in the US, is marketed by the Saxone division of Clore's British Shoe Corporation; American Tuf and Rogues shoes are also marketed through retail footwear chain stores. The Gluv range is the first medium priced footwear to contain the American Du Pont's Corfam uppers. These shoes are made by G B Britton, a UK concern. The American company Genesco has a 35 per cent investment in Rayne/Delman, well-known shoe manufacturers which operate a number of retail outlets.

Actifresh, the deodorant treatment for clothes is being used in a number of applications. Freeman-Horn has obtained exclusive rights to treat its Skinfit shoe linings with the product.

Bally Shoes, with a large factory in Norwich, is a subsidiary of the Swiss parent (the majority of its board of directors are Swiss); the shops London Shoe Company and Russell & Bromley are also Bally subsidiaries. Foot comfort is almost synonymous with Scholl, entirely American owned.

Over 80 per cent of the shoe machinery market is held by British United Shoe Machinery owned by the United Shoe Machinery Corporation of Boston which has further strengthened its British interests by acquiring the business formerly carried on by Light Sons & Williams, manufacturers of stereo-moulding presses and related machinery. United Shoe has also acquired, with Turner Machinery of Leeds, John Orme specialists in rotational-moulding machinery. British United Shoe is currently expanding its precision-plastic mouldings factory at Stockton-on-Tees.

Courtaulds' share of the women's stockings and lingerie market is about 20 per cent; a well-known American company active in hosiery manufacture is Berkshire International with a factory in Newtownards. Elbeo, a German company, also manufactures hosiery in the UK.

Pretty Polly, the stockings manufacturer in the Thomas Tilling Group, is in process of forming a Swiss company in conjunction with two American concerns to handle the world rights in Leprechauns, the stretch-stocking technique. The American companies are Hanes, a market leader in the US and Hin, a small prestige hosiery firm.

Marks & Spencer's St Michael has almost a third of the market for brassieres and foundation garments but American interests are well represented. Lovable, whose parent company is in Georgia, claims some 13 per cent of the brassiere market. Playtex, a subsidiary of International Playtex of Delaware, has just over nine per cent. It also manufactures foundation garments under the brand name Sarongster. Berlei, with some six per cent is a subsidiary of an Australian parent company. The German Triumph corsetry is also popular in Britain. The American Maidenform has just pulled out of the UK foundation market industry, no longer having a licence to manufacture. Spencer (Banbury) which is well-known for surgical corsetry is an American firm.

7

HOUSEHOLD PRODUCTS INCLUDING
APPLIANCES, CLEANERS AND PACKAGING

Leading overseas companies active in the manufacture of domestic household appliances include the Anglo-Dutch Philips, the Swedish Electrolux and the American Hoover and Frigidaire; these together with British Domestic Appliances (the UK group consisting of GEC/AEI, Morphy Richards and EMI) account for a majority of domestic appliances bought in Britain. The US General Telephone has disposed of its small stake in Thorn.

Electrolux has about 11 per cent of the refrigerator market currently worth more than £20 million. Tricity, a British (Thorn) brand, has nine per cent and the next most popular makes are Hoover and Frigidaire, the domestic appliances division of General Motors. Kelvinator, formerly an American Motors subsidiary which has just been acquired by White Consolidated Industries, another US firm, also sells refrigerators. As well as manufacturing its own range of refrigerators, Hoover markets the Italian Zanussi refrigerator.

Europe's largest refrigerator makers, Ignis of Milan, recently launched a cut-price campaign in Britain. In a deal with Currys, the chain store, the Italians offer refrigerators and deep freeze units at prices well below those recommended by British manufacturers. Ignis plans to sell 10,000 to 20,000 models in Britain during 1968 under its own brand name, in addition to the substantial volume it already sells under the Philips label at considerably higher prices.

At the lower end of the price range the company will be in direct conflict with Indesit, another Italian refrigerator manufacturer. In 1967

Indesit sold some 60,000 models in Britain, taking six per cent of the market.

Frigoscandia, the British subsidiary of the Malmros Shipping Company of Sweden will shortly be introducing the prototype of a prefabricated 'back room' cold store plant for retailers and caterers. Frigoscandia, formerly known as Northern Cold Storage, has more than seven million cubic feet of controlled temperature storage in Britain, about eight per cent of the total of this industrial market. Its customers include Birds Eye and Ross. The Swedish investment in this country since the company began its UK operations in 1958 is £4 million. This figure is expected to double within five years as the company intends to set up at least three more storage depots.

The largest producer of commercial refrigeration is York Shipley, a division of the Borg-Warner Corporation of Chicago.

Hoover, of course, is best known for its vacuum cleaners which hold almost 60 per cent of the market. The company has been manufacturing in Britain since 1931, and has 30 per cent or more of the washing machine market and a 28 per cent share for spin and tumbler dryers under its trade names Hoovermatic, Keymatic and Spinarinse. Hoover is now manufacturing gas fires and is expected to enter the gas cooker market shortly. The GEC/AEI complex is a strong contender in washing machines, Hotpoint claiming 25 per cent and Frigidaire 14 per cent. Another popular machine is made by Ada of Halifax, the Philips subsidiary which also manufactures electric irons. There are a number of imported spin dryers on the market mainly from Western Germany.

One of the largest companies manufacturing industrial laundry equipment is British Laundry Machine Company, a subsidiary of McGraw-Edison of Illinois. A large amount of laundry and dry cleaning equipment is imported, Polymark acting as agents for a number of overseas lines. The German Poensgen, a leading maker of continuous washing machines, has a factory in Britain. Manlove Alliott holds the licence for an American washer extractor. Kelvinator is active in the coin-op washing machine field; this equipment is distributed in the UK by Gomoco.

Dishwashers show the British Colston well to the fore, with Hoover also popular. The German Bosch has recently begun to penetrate this market. Hobart Manufacturing whose parent company is in Ohio, also makes dishwashers and food preparation machines.

Waste disposal units are just beginning to gain favour in Britain with the US In-sink-erator having ten per cent of the market.

Food mixers are the province of British Kenwood, with the French Moulinex also popular. Moulinex dominates the market for coffee mills taking some three-quarters of it. The company does not manufacture in Britain but is distributed by Andrews Housewares. Morphy Richards is the next most popular make of coffee mill, followed by the German Braun and the French Rallye. Henning Glahn distributes the Braun products and Rudson Wood acts as the Rallye distributor.

Proctor-Silex, part of the Smith Corona Marchant Corporation of

America, is introducing four of its Whiteline brand of domestic appliances to the British market in September 1968. The products are a coffee percolator, a toaster and two types of steam iron. It is expected that the products will ultimately be made in this country at West Bromwich to supply both the British and European markets.

Originally known mainly on account of its lamps and lighting appliances, Philips recently took over Pye of Cambridge and now has across-the-board interests ranging from gramophone records to radio and television apparatus and scientific instruments. The radio, television and record-playing equipment division of Philips accounts for about a quarter of group sales. At its Eindhoven headquarters Philips manufactures colour television sets for all three prevailing systems. The two service organisations of Philips and Pye have been merged to form Combined Electronic Services which will ultimately become responsible for after-sales service and spares for all radio, television and domestic appliances marketed by the two merged companies.

British interests are still strong in domestic appliances. Through its alliance with AEI, GEC acquired a 50 per cent ownership of Thorn-AEI radio valves and tubes and a similar 50 per cent ownership of British Domestic Appliances. Added to this GEC/AEI has 35 per cent of British Lighting Industries with Thorn controlling the majority. British Lighting Industries has a strong hold on radio and television sets but is strongly challenged by the Philips-Pye group which now claims 25 per cent of the British television set market. Philips manufactures under the brand names Dynatron, Mullard, Stella, Pye, Ecko and Ferranti; GEC makes the Sobell, Masteradio and McMichael sets. Standard Telephones & Cables (a subsidiary of the American ITT) is strongly placed with KB, Regentone and RGD. The Ford Motor Company's subsidiary Philco also manufactures radio and television sets.

The PAL colour television system which has been adopted in the UK was pioneered by Dr Walter Bruch of West Germany. The Radio Corporation of America, pioneers of colour TV in the United States had negotiated a colour television manufacturing arrangement with Radio Rentals which involved an initial investment in Britain of £2 million. This arrangement could well be upset by the merger between Radio Rentals and Thorn.

Electric blankets are the province of the British GEC which has 50 per cent of the market; the American brand Monogram, made by General Electric of America, takes a further 35 per cent.

The GEC/AEI link-up has increased the latter's share of gas and electric cookers. GEC probably has one-fifth of the electric cooker market and, through its Cannon subsidiary, something around eight per cent of gas cooker sales. Westinghouse, the New York company with a London subsidiary, is popular in the higher priced range of electric cookers.

Market leaders in electric light bulbs are British Lighting Industries (in which GEC has an interest); GEC/Osram; Aladdin which is American owned; and Philips.

Best Products, a subsidiary of the British A C Cossor and the Raytheon

Company of Massachusetts makes a wide range of kettles, toasters, coffee percolators and other household appliances.

The small batteries used in deaf aids, cameras, clocks and watches are mainly made by the American owned Mallory whose recent price increase caused censure by the Prices & Incomes Board.

The largest sales of rotary lawn mowers in Britain belong to the Swedish Flymo.

Sewing machines show Singer holding 40 per cent of the market, Singer has had a factory in Scotland since 1882 and is 87 per cent owned by the New York company. The company also manufactures refrigerators and distributes an Italian-made range. Brother, a Japanese brand with a good distribution in department stores, sells under its own name and also supplies machines for private label brands, for example Curry's Westminster brand is a Brother model. The Italian Necchi and the German Pfaff also sell well in the higher priced market. The Pfaff British agent is Willcox & Gibbs an American subsidiary which itself is a leading manufacturer of industrial sewing machines. Union Special Machine, again American owned, is another large manufacturer of industrial sewing machines.

The Prestige Group is owned by American Home Products Corporation of New York. Prestige dominates the kitchen knives and housewares market; it makes the Skyline range of household products as well as Ewbank carpet sweepers, O-Cedar and Happimaid mops and the company has recently introduced a range of small appliances produced by Edison of the USA.

Halex is known for Bex and Bex-Bissell carpet sweepers and carpet shampoos. Halex is a division of Bakelite-Xylonite, the company jointly owned by Distillers and Union Carbide. Bissell is a licensing agreement Halex operates for Bissell Inc of Michigan.

British cutlery still holds the majority of the market although the American Oneida which manufactures in Northern Ireland has become an active producer of high quality silver plate and stainless cutlery. Colly Products and Pal Personna are both American controlled, the latter being part of Philip Morris, have both penetrated the cutlery industry. Crown Staffordshire China and Enoch Wedgewood are two subsidiaries of Seymart Importing Company of New York; the American Carborundum owns Copeland, the firm which makes Spode china.

Thermos is almost a generic name but in fact 40 different vacuum flasks and jugs are made at Brentford by the company which is a subsidiary of King-Seeley Thermos Co of Ann Arbor. Thermos is an active supporter of the campaign to back British goods and has a fine export record. It produces ten million vacuum flasks a year, exports about 55 per cent and claims to have a 60 per cent share of the market; the company also makes its own glass vacuum bottles at Thetford. Another large manufacturer of vacuum flasks is Aladdin Industries, owned by an American parent in Nashville.

The Tupperware range of plastic household containers which are sold by direct methods is owned by the American Rexall Drug Laboratories through its Tupperware subsidiary.

A number of European companies distribute table and glassware in the UK – Rosenthal China is German, Gero is Dutch and Scandinavian designs such as Orefors glass are sold in Britain through distributors.

Detergent interests show strong overseas investments. Current market shares give Unilever (Dutch/British) about 45 per cent of the market and the American owned Procter & Gamble some 43 per cent. A tabulated look at the more familiar trade names in the detergents, cleansers and soap powders fields indicates their manufacturers:

Type	Unilever products	Procter & Gamble products
Heavy duty soap powders	*Persil (28%)* *Rinso* *Omo (15%)* *Surf (5%)*	*Fairy Snow (13%)* *Soap Oxydol* *Daz (18%)* *Tide (11%)* *Blue Oxydol*
Light duty washing products: *Soap flakes* *Synthetic powders* *Synthetic liquids*	*Lux* *Stergene*	 *Dreft*
Washing-up liquids	*Lux liquid (11%)* *Quix (12%)* *Sqezy (17%)*	*Fairy liquid (34%)* *Liquid Dreft* *(test marketed only)*
Household cleaners	*Dual (27%)* *Handy Andy (13%)*	*Flash (34%)*
Bleach	*Domestos (33%)*	
Abrasives	*Vim (41%)*	*Mirro*

(approximate market shares in brackets)

Unilever also owns Thames Board Mills which makes the group's carton and board cases.

Colgate-Palmolive, another wholly-owned American subsidiary which started British operations in 1922, is responsible for the washing powders Fab and Ola, as well as Ajax, the household abrasive cleanser, which holds about half the market for this type of scouring product.

Swipe, a concentrated detergent which is sold by housewives and part-time workers with great success in the USA, its country of origin, recently began British operations. Already the company musters a part-time sales force of 7,000.

Economics Laboratory of Minnesota is about to market a washing-up detergent called Finish, the product is already well-established in Europe.

Both Unilever and Procter & Gamble have launched enzyme-based washing powders, Unilever with Radiant and Drive, Procter & Gamble with Ariel.

Grange Chemicals which supplies almost the entire industry with detergent base is part-owned by BP with two-thirds and Chevron with a one-third share. Calgon the water softener, now owned by Merck, is an American product. Its licensee is Albright & Wilson.

Oven cleansers show Phillips, Scott & Turner's Shift a clear market leader. Phillips, Scott & Turner, which also manufactures Big S stain remover is owned by the Sterling-Winthrop group. S C Johnson's Force is the next most popular brand; this company's parent is in Wisconsin. It makes a wide range of wax polishes, air fresheners and disinfectants. Johnson recently acquired the Leicester firm J Goddard. Other American subsidiaries active in the field of polishes include Simoniz with a Chicago head office and Silicone Processes, a Monsanto subsidiary. Lloyd's Industries markets the American Turtle Wax car polish. Stanley Home Products, the Wisconsin company which specialises in the direct sale of household polishes, mops and brushes, is about to open in the UK.

Airwick and Airfresh are both made by Airkem of New Jersey and Brillo the steel wool people are owned by the Purex Corporation whose headquarters are in California.

Household foil is made by Aluminium Foils under the trade name Baco. Aluminium Foils is owned by Reynolds Metals of America (51 per cent) and the British Tube Investments (49 per cent). Alcan is a Canadian subsidiary; Impalco is made by Imperial Aluminium, 75 per cent owned by the Aluminium Company of Chicago and the rest by Norway's Elektrokemisk; British Aluminium, also active in the production of household foils is owned by Tube Investments (48 per cent) and Reynolds Metals (48 per cent).

BXL, the company jointly owned by Union Carbide and Distillers manufactures polythene film and plastic bags and boxes under its trade name Bexthene. Flexer Paper Sacks is owned by a Swedish concern. Monsanto supplies the packaging industry with raw materials in quantity.

British Sidac, which manufactures packaging materials and cellulose film is controlled by the Belgian Financière de la Cellulose (39·62 per cent of the equity), together with British American Tobacco and Imperial Tobacco via the jointly owned company Mardon International (37·83 per cent of the equity). In April 1968 British Sidac set up a joint company, Sidex, with ICI to manufacture polypropylene film for the packaging market. Sidac holds 51 per cent of the capital.

British Sisalkraft, 70 per cent of whose capital is owned by the British subsidiary of St Regis Paper of New York, also makes a wide range of paper and waterproof papers both for the packaging and building industries.

Amalgamated Packaging Industries is another London-based St Regis subsidiary.

Fasson Products, a subsidiary of Avery Production Corporation of California, is well known for self-adhesive papers, packaging film and foils. Crown Cork, whose metal cap activities were briefly noted in the food and drink section of this book, also manufactures aerosols and containers. Its parent is Crown Cork & Seal of Philadelphia.

Beginning to find its way into many British kitchens is the Ziehfix can which eliminates the need for a tin opener. This is manufactured by the Metal Box Company under licence.

Mirroware is a cross licensing agreement between Mirro Aluminium of Wisconsin and the British concern of the same name.

Schiedamsche Lederwarenfabriek of Tilburg, Holland, is building a Lanarkshire factory. Together with its new Scottish subsidiary Intercase, the company will manufacture presentation cases for electric shavers and also leather cases for other instruments.

Wrapping paper is a British stronghold with the Reed Paper Group, Bowater, E S & A Robinson and Wiggins Teape the main manufacturers. An Anglo-American co-operation is effected by Mead Robinson, a joint subsidiary of Robinson and the Mead Corporation of Ohio. Robinson also has a joint subsidiary, Keyes Robinson, set up with Keyes Fibre of Maine which sells moulded pulp products.

Cartons show the British companies Reed, Bowater, Metal Box, Robinson, Waddington and Tillotson the most important manufacturers. Austin Packaging, owned by Thames Board Mills, a Unilever subsidiary, has a small share of the market. Pembroke Carton & Printing is jointly owned by Ilford (which itself is part Swiss controlled) and Carreras.

An Anglo-American collaboration in the field of containers is that of Tri-Wall Containers which was formed by Tillotsons with Tri-Wall Containers of New York. Universal Container, another active concern in this sphere of operations has a parent company located in New York; ITW which makes plastic containers is a subsidiary of Illinois Tool Works.

International Packaging, an American owned company, makes a wide range of presentation boxes; Cooks Corrugated Cases is a subsidiary of the Canadian MacMillan, Bloedel & Powell River. Ulster Paper Producers, which also makes corrugated boxes, is a subsidiary of the St Joe Paper Corporation of Florida. Corrugated Products, which manufactures cartons and sleeves is Canadian owned. John Thompson makes containers under licence from the Pullman Corporation of Chicago.

British Cellophane's subsidiary Colodense has an exchange agreement with American Can for the development and introduction of new flexible packaging materials for the British market. Cellophane wrapping material is made by British Cellophane in association with the French Rhône-Poulenc. British Cellophane itself is owned by Courtaulds whose cans, drums and metal boxes interests are handled by Reads, the Liverpool firm which Courtaulds set up jointly with American Can.

Owens-Illinois, the Ohio company probably produces more bottles and jars a year than any other single producer in the world. Owens-Illinois has a 16 per cent share in United Glass. The American company sends accumulated know-how to United Glass receiving in return payments in the region of £300,000 a year in addition to its shareholding. Under the terms of the technical assistance agreement, signed in 1966 for a minimum period of ten years, United Glass is committed to pay Owens-Illinois annual amounts equivalent to $1\frac{1}{4}$ per cent of its turnover on glass containers. Two Owens-Illinois directors serve on the United Glass board.

United Glass is the leading glass container manufacturer in the UK with just under 40 per cent of the market. Its nearest competitor is Rockware which itself has an agreement with the American Wheaton Glass Company to produce and sell US designed small glass containers. Rockware is emerging as the leading manufacturer of the one-trip mineral bottle. Rockware's subsidiaries are Garston Bottle, Forster's Glass and Blewis & Shaw. The latter company has a know-how arrangement with a Japanese firm which so far has only resulted in Japanese income for the British company.

James A Jobling manufactures the Pyrex range of glassware. This company is 60 per cent owned by the British Thomas Tilling the remaining 40 per cent of its capital is owned by the Corning Glass of New York, nearest American rival to Owens-Illinois.

8

BANKING, FINANCE AND PROPERTY

Since London is the banking centre of the world it is not surprising to find more than 100 overseas banks with British offices and these foreign banks account for 34 per cent of net deposits with banks in the UK.

Among countries represented by banking interests in Britain are Spain, Portugal, Israel, USA, Canada, New Zealand, Ceylon, Belgium, France, Holland, India, Turkey, Greece and Japan. By the far largest number of entrants has come from the USA which had only seven banks with branches here in 1958 as against nearly 20 now, although banks such as Morgan Guaranty, Hanover Trust and First National City have been in London since the beginning of the century. Deposits held by US banks in London have increased from £389 million in 1960 to £3,927 million by the end of March 1968. Advances have risen even more steeply. In fact gross deposits of the foreign and overseas banks in London are now rising so rapidly that they will soon rival those of the clearing banks.

Since the latest figures were published several more USA banks have continued the trans-Atlantic trend. The oldest American bank, the First Pennsylvania Banking & Trust Company which was set up in 1782 and claims to be the twentieth largest in the US, has opened a representative office at 38 Wallbrook EC4. This was instigated largely because London is the centre of the Euro-dollar market and it is thought that First Pennsylvania will eventually convert its representative office into a branch. The United California Bank is about to establish permanent London headquarters in a new building in Moorgate. The Mellon National Bank & Trust Company of Pittsburgh recently chose London for the first of its

European operations and this branch is located in Moorgate. Kuhn Loeb has also opened a branch to concentrate in Eurobond new issue and stock exchange business and the National Bank of Commerce of Seattle is another new arrival to the London banking scene.

Three American banks – Wells Fargo, National Bank of Detroit and Security First National – have joined with Hambros in a joint venture called Western American Bank (Europe) which has enabled them to share the cost of opening a London branch. This trend may well spread to other smaller us banks.

As well as from America, there has also been a significant flow of banking interests from Switzerland, Japan, Pakistan and France.

Korea Exchange Bank now has a London branch, the Israel-British Bank of Tel Aviv has formed a British subsidiary and a group of five Scandinavian banks plan to set up a London office, probably in co-operation with a British bank.

Julius Baer International is a new bank which recently began London operations. Of this bank 51 per cent is owned by Fibena AG, a Swiss holding company closely connected with Julius Baer, themselves Swiss bankers. Of the London branch 49 per cent is owned by International Finance & Services, the overseas trade finance subsidiary of United Dominions Trust.

Merchant bankers Henry Ansbacher recently sold a 30 per cent share stake to North Carolina's Wachovia Bank & Trust Company (20 per cent) and the New York based Zilka & Sons financial group (10 per cent). The American shareholding will be increased in the long term and both sides acknowledge that control of Ansbacher could eventually pass to the Americans. Wachovia is thirty-ninth in the American banking world with assets of £583 million.

Twenty-five per cent of E D Sasson Banking is owned by Continental Illinois National Bank & Trust of Chicago; the First National City Bank of New York has a substantial shareholding in Hill, Samuel.

The Texas National Bank of Commerce has bought a 35 per cent stake in Burston, a small merchant bank until recently controlled by Mr Neville Burston and the Howard de Walden family. Manufacturers Hanover Trust holds a majority interest in Manufacturers Hanover, a new merchant bank in which Rothschilds and a Milan insurance company – Riunione Adriatica di Sicurta – also participate. Brown Brothers Harriman, which claims to be America's largest private bank, has bought a share in Fleming-Suez which was set up in early 1968 by London merchant bankers Robert Fleming and the Compagnie Financière de Suez et de l'Union (the former Suez Canal Co).

A number of unit trusts offer investments in overseas stock. One such is Pan Australian which specialises, as its name implies, in Australian investment.

The leading American firm of stockbrokers Merrill Lynch, Pierce, Fenner & Smith has two offices in London. This is the only firm of stockbrokers which takes advertising space in the *Financial Times* and other papers. The Stock Exchange does not allow British registered stockbrokers to advertise their services at present.

Other American stockbrokers with London offices include Bache & Co; Baker, Weeks; Dominick & Dominick; Francis I DuPont; Estabrook of Boston; Loeb, Rhoades and H Hentz the international commodity brokers.

Diners' Club, one of the leading credit card operations is owned 56 per cent by the American Diners' Club and 40 per cent by the Westminster Bank. Diners cards are accepted internationally and Diners' Club has a fully-owned subsidiary called Cardholder Services which provides a service to those businesses which issue credit cards and have accounting systems.

Dun & Bradstreet, the company famous for its reports on company status and offering general investment services, is American owned. In 1964 Dun & Bradstreet acquired the capital of both Stubbs and Moodies Services. Dun & Bradstreet publishes directories and a quarterly business journal.

Another American owned investment service primarily for stockbrokers is the Dow Jones New Service with an active London office.

Reuters, the international news agency, which has a partnership with Ultronic Systems Corporation of America, is controlled by a trust and owned by London, regional, Australian and New Zealand newspapers. United Press International, another news service, is owned by UPI of New York. The controlling interest is held by Scripps-Howard Newspapers.

Mercantile Credit Company is one of the foremost leasing concerns in Britain; the United States Leasing Corporation holds a 20 per cent stake in Mercantile's subsidiary Mercantile Leasing and the American company's former chairman has been elected to the board of the British company.

The American Express Company is probably best known in the field of travel. In fact the company is a financial trust and one of its subsidiaries is Hertz American Express International which it owns jointly with the Hertz Corporation.

H & H Factors, one of the largest factoring organisations, is a subsidiary of Walter E Heller of Chicago; Unifinance, which specialises in financing industrial equipment is a subsidiary of CIT; Beneficial Finance & Seabord Surity, both of which handle surity bonds are American owned. Two other American companies active in investment securities and as underwriters and distributors are Hallgarten & Co and Kidder, Peabody. Hirsch is a large New York firm of securities and commodities brokers which also has a London office.

Some 25 overseas insurance companies have offices in Britain. One of the latest arrivals is the Australian Mutual Provident Society which has assets of £850 million. Australian, Canadian, New Zealand, Danish and Swiss interests are strongly represented. American assurance companies also have interests in British concerns. For example Phoenix Insurance is backed by the US Continental Insurance which holds 25 per cent of its equity. Bishopsgate Insurance is a subsidiary of Mobil Oil.

Nationale-Nederlanden, Holland's largest insurance company, whose gross assets total £665 million has acquired the Life Association of Scotland, the Dutch company already has a 46 per cent stake in Orion Insurance. Geneva-based Investors Overseas Services is expanding its UK activities in addition to the full range of Dover Plan life policies now handled by the company's existing British subsidiary, International Life Insurance. The parent holding company of IOS is registered in Panama.

Other American assurance companies with London subsidiaries include Abbey Life, one of the pioneers of unit-trust linked assurance schemes, whose parent is Great International Life; Occidental Life Insurance Company of North Carolina; Dominion-Lincoln, whose parent company is Lincoln National Life of Fort Wayne; American Continental Life; Insurance Company of North America and Crawford & Co, the insurance claims adjusters and assessors, whose head office is in Atlanta.

A number of overseas finance companies have London branches amongst which are two Canadians: James Richardson and Royal Trust. Greenhaven Securities, particularly active in property and estate management, is partly controlled by a South African company. Plus Flats which owns a number of large blocks of flats in the greater London area is owned by Freshwater, an American concern.

The £57 million Dalgety & New Zealand Loan Co, a famous name in Australasia has a £3 million investment in East Anglia under the name Dalgety Franklin. It hopes to build a business based on supplying farmers with agricultural requirements and is currently on the look-out for agricultural merchants and agricultural engineering firms.

GRAMCO, the management company for an international property fund, US Investment Fund, is to establish its headquarters in London. The fund's chairman is Pierre Salinger, former White House press secretary. The fund is based in Nassau.

9
OFFICE EQUIPMENT AND
DATA PROCESSING

There is virtually no British owned typewriter industry. Imperial Typewriter is a subsidiary of Litton Industries, the American company which also owns Royal McBee and has an estimated 30 per cent share of the manuals market. Imperial recently produced a new American designed electric model as the first fruits of its merger with Litton.

Since it acquired the American Underwood, Italy's Olivetti, after closing down the Underwood factory in Brighton, has concentrated its Glasgow factory on standard manual machines and imports portables and electric models from its Italian parent. Olivetti is expanding its Glasgow plant which currently exports a large proportion of its output. British Olivetti started in 1947 and now employs 1,600. The international company of which it is part is rated the third largest office equipment firm in the world, and plans to introduce the sale of copying machines in the UK.

In the area of electric typewriters, the American IBM has a third of the market, then comes British Olivetti (15 per cent) and another American company SCM (formerly Smith-Corona). SCM also manufactures portables at its North Wales factory; its British head office is at West Bromwich from where a large proportion of its machines are exported.

Olympia is owned by the German AEG (Allgemeine Elektricitätsgesellschaft). Remington-Rand, a division of the American Sperry Rand, now concentrates its typewriter division in Holland and Italy having closed down its Glasgow plant.

A number of foreign typewriters are imported into the UK including the Swiss Hermes and the Japanese Brother and Sterling. It is perhaps ironic that the only major British owned company, Office & Electronic Machines confines itself to selling the German Adler range of typewriters.

Imports of office machinery of all types run at a high level as indicated by the following United Nations statistics:

United Kingdom imports of office equipment

	(Value in thousands of US dollars)	
	1965	*1966*
Office machines, total	148,707	237,054
United States	74,608	90,481
West Germany	28,254	63,457
France	18,531	41,913
Other countries	27,314	41,113
Typewriters, check writers, total	19,657	21,407
West Germany	10,148	10,269
Netherlands	3,556	3,546
Italy	1,840	2,773
Other countries	4,113	4,819
Accounting machines, computers, total	21,820	29,373
United States	6,007	10,371
West Germany	4,332	5,200
Sweden	3,839	3,763
Other countries	7,642	10,039
Statistical machines, total	47,401	91,825
West Germany	10,742	36,616
United States	21,719	26,081
France	11,958	18,843
Other countries	2,982	10,285
Miscellaneous office machines, total	59,829	94,448
United States	45,406	51,452
France	6,077	22,614
West Germany	3,033	11,462
Other countries	5,313	8,920

Source: United Nations: Commodity Trade Statistics.

In the field of reprographic equipment Kodak, owned by Eastman Kodak, has the biggest single share of the British market with the Minnesota Mining & Manufacturing Company, Bell & Howell and A B Dick, all American owned concerns, high among its competitors. For electrostatic copying Rank Xerox, which is jointly owned by the Rank Organisation and the Xerox Corporation of New York is the dominant company, being challenged by further Americans in the shape of scm, Addressograph-Multigraph, Apeco (whose parent is the American Photocopy Equipment Company of Illinois) and Copycat owned by the Nashua Corporation. Block & Anderson markets a number of imported models; Ilford, part Swiss owned, and Remington-Rand also manufacture a range of photo-copying machines. Lines Bros, the Triang toy firm is about to launch an American-designed copying machine known as the CopyMate. This is the first machine to be specifically designed for home and school use; origin-ally a 3M product, the rights are now owned by an American toy com-pany called Transogram and the agreement with Lines will give the British firm manufacturing and sales rights for Commonwealth and EFTA countries.

Microfilm equipment is the province of Kodak, Minnesota Mining and the Reprographic Products Division of GAF (Great Britain) which also handles a number of imported microfilm cameras, readers and printers. Formerly called Hall Harding, this subsidiary of General Aniline & Film Corporation of New York, is well known in the field of drawing office equipment and graphic arts supplies.

Micro Methods markcts a range of German microfilm cameras; Remington-Rand makes a planetary engineering camera, and about to be marketed in Britain is the National Cash Register's PMCI microfilm system which achieves reductions of 40,000:1. Readex Microprint, an American owned concern makes a microfilm viewer and another active manufac-turer of microfilm equipment is Bell & Howell. This company, with its headquarters in Chicago, has three divisions in the UK active in photo-graphy, electronic instruments and vacuum equipment. University Micro-film, another Xerox subsidiary, specialises in microfilm and xerographic reproduction.

Addressograph-Multigraph manufactures an electrostatic enlarger printer and a range of addressing machines. The company employs more than 2,000 and three of its four directors are American. Its other trade names include Multilith, Cardograph, Dupligraph and Systemat. A sub-sidiary of Addressograph-Multigraph is Admel International, a large manufacturer and supplier of drawing office equipment, printing machines and photographic chemicals. A further division is Varityper which re-cently introduced a new phototypesetting machine into the UK designed by the Photon Corporation of Massachusetts.

The American National Cash Register, whose London offices house the 'I'm backing Britain' campaign claims to have more cash registers in use in Britain than any other company. NCR is also strongly placed in account-ing machines. Facit, the Swedish group which operates through Block & Anderson for its UK marketing has some 15 per cent of the market. Facit has just announced that it will manufacture in Britain, a factory near Rochester is envisaged. The Swedish owned Addo; the Norwegian Adwel, the German Anker, and Monroe and Sweda, two more Litton Industries' subsidiaries, are further examples of overseas investments in calculating machines.

In electronic calculators, National Cash Register and Burroughs are the American market leaders with a strong challenger in Anglo-Dutch Philips' recently acquired Logabax range, which is now known as Philips Electrologica. Philips is also launching a range of computing devices and business machines and will shortly be entering the field of automatic type-writers, invoicing machines and visible record units. Philips markets the German Siemag range of electronic business equipment, but it is under-stood that these will be manufactured in Britain at a later date.

At the beginning of 1968 marketing and servicing of the Aristocrat range of accounting machines passed from Remington-Rand to a new UK concern called Kienzle Data Systems. This company is a subsidiary of the West German manufacturers of the same name. Friden, distributors of electronic invoicing machines, is a division of the American Singer. Friden also markets its parent company's data collection systems, a low-cost desk computer and automatic writing machines under the trade name Flexo-writer. The American owned Hewlett Packard has recently introduced a programmable electronic calculator which performs operations commonly encountered in scientfiic and engineering problems.

Think of dictating machines and the chances are you will think of the German Grundig. The Grundig plant in Northern Ireland manufactures a wide range of tape recorders and dictating machines and 61 per cent of this factory's output is exported. Other well known names in the field of tape recorders and dictating machines are Philips, IBM, Bosch and Olympia, the last two being West German. The Swedish Aga now manufactures in Britain and the company handling the Agavox range has recently changed the spelling of its name to Agovox, a necessary consequence of Swedish trade mark regulations. Ultravox is another important range of dictating machines which are made by Gutar Holdings of Switzerland. Until recently British distribution of Ultravox was handled by Remington-Rand. However Ultravox has just been taken over by the Dictaphone Company which is now responsible for the distribution of Ultravox equipment. Dictaphone, whose parent company is in New York, recently acquired the London office services firm Norma Skemp as part of a diversi-fying programme. The Norma Skemp organisation offers a wide range of services including the supply of temporary secretarial help, printing, design and duplicating facilities, translations and the like.

Vending machines are mainly supplied by British manufacturers such as Ditchburn and British Automatic. American interests represented in the sphere of automated canteen services include Vendepac a division of Mars; ITW's Conex division whose parent is Illinois Tool Works; and Lily Cups & Containers which operates under a licensing agreement from the American concern of the same name.

The largest firm of addressing machines is Addressograph-Multigraph the American owned company which, as we have seen, also makes office printing machines, photo-composing and duplicating equipment. Elliott

Business Machines, a subsidiary of Dymo Industries of California, both manufactures and distributes a range of addressing and listing equipment. Adrema, which has plants at Acton and Cosham is also active in this area; Bradma is one of the machines it makes. Adrema is a subsidiary of Farrington Manufacturing, the Swedish Citograf is also part of the Farrington group. Besides data processing and printing equipment Farrington produces voice-print equipment which can provide identification by means of spectrographic voice examination and the group has also acquired the manufacturing and marketing rights for the credit register originated by Telecredit of Los Angeles. This unit will imprint and recognise limits on credit cards and carry out regular up-dating.

Pitney-Bowes, whose parent is located in Stamford, Connecticut, is the leading manufacturer of postal franking, mailing, letter sealing, folding and opening machines. Postage & Revenue Franking Machines which has just over five per cent of Britain's franking machine market sells a Swiss-made machine. Lamson Industries, the British firm which dominates business forms, has a minority cross-shareholding arrangement with the Moore Corporation of Toronto.

Art Metal, manufacturers of steel furniture, filing equipment and strip indexes, is an American subsidiary; Acco, another large manufacturer and supplier of office equipment including punches and folders, has its parent company located in Chicago. The largest manufacturer of binding equipment, General Binding, is also American owned.

Creed, the teleprinter and data processing equipment company is a subsidiary of International Telephone & Telegraph. Creed's teleprinter has been accepted as the standard machine for the UK telex network which is ordered in quantity by the GPO. Telex subscribers currently number 22,000 and the demand for this system increases by some 20 per cent a year.

Answering, manufacturers of telephone answering equipment, is a subsidiary of the Washington company of the same name. Ampex, which manufactures a range of magnetic recording equipment is American owned as is Magnavox which is also active in sound recording and reproducing equipment and components.

Muzak, the system for piped music in factories and offices is American; the biggest security firm outside America is Group 4 (formerly Factory-guards) which is owned by Bevaknings AB Securitas of Mälmo. The Group currently imports a range of security equipment and alarm systems from Sweden but will shortly be manufacturing this equipment in Britain. Group 4 employs 1,600 in this country. Electric Protection Services is the UK subsidiary of American District Telegraph.

Photo-Scan, the British subsidiary of the American group, has introduced a device invented to discourage shoplifting. Photo-Scan operates on a franchise basis at present but is shortly to start manufacture at Shepperton.

Remploy, the organisation which gives employment to the disabled, is best known for its Lundia range of equipment. Lundia shelving is in fact the result of a licence agreement with H Lundquist of Geneva.

General Time Corporation of Connecticut has two British subsidiaries: Ether-Haydon concerned with industrial timing devices and owned jointly with Ether of Stevenage; and General Time which has a Dumbarton factory engaged in watch and clock manufacture.

Two popular marking systems are both American owned; Weber-Fanfold whose parent is in Illinois, and Markem with a head office in New Hampshire.

Avery Adhesive Products which opened a factory in Cumbernauld in 1963 is well-known for its adhesive labels. Its parent company is located in California.

Henry C Stephens, makers of inks, carbon papers, ribbons, pens, stapling machines and a range of office accessories, has some 67 per cent of its ordinary capital owned by a Delaware company. The Carter's Ink Company of the US has just formed a British subsidiary based in Peckham to make industrial and commercial markers and stationery items. Another leading manufacturer of inked ribbons and carbon papers is the American owned Columbia Ribbon & Carbon Manufacturing Company. Bostich, manufacturers of industrial and office stapling equipment, is owned by the Bostich Division of Textron in Rhode Island.

Two major American companies and Wiggins Teape, the big UK paper-maker, co-operate on the marketing of carbonless papers in Europe. The US companies are National Cash Register and the Minnesota Mining & Manufacturing Company. Wiggins Teape is the NCR licensee and makes NCR paper at plants in South Wales and Belgium. It has a non-exclusive licence to sell the product anywhere in the world outside the USA. Under the terms of the revised agreement Wiggins Teape makes NCR paper available to 3M for sale in Europe. In return 3M supplies its carbonless paper to Wiggins Teape for sale in Europe. 3M is also well known for its Scotch adhesive and recording tape.

Ninety-five per cent of the world market for computers lies in the hands of American companies. IBM has almost 60 per cent of the world market; then comes Univac, part of the Sperry Rand Group; Honeywell and Burroughs, both American controlled are also fully operational in the UK.

The largest British computer manufacturer is International Computers.

The present ownership of International Computers also raises some interesting questions. At one time the Vickers division of Sperry Rand had a large shareholding in ICT through its Powers ownership. (Sperry Rand is itself the parent company of Univac and its Vickers division should not be confused with the all-British engineering concern). This formerly approached 50 per cent. Vickers shareholding has since been substantially reduced and is now probably in the order of 17 per cent. Under the merger of ICT with English Electric the shareholding is of somewhat less significance.

Of the computer systems manufactured in Great Britain, a considerable amount originate from America, both in the form of complete peripheral devices such as magnetic tape units, disc files, line printers and the like.

Similar devices, in particular magnetic tape units, come from France and other European sources. Other peripheral devices are ostensibly manufactured in Britain but in reality these are assembled from sizeable unit parts which are of overseas, mainly American, manufacture and the actual British content is relatively small.

The current earning position of computer manufacturers in the UK

Company	Country of origin	Sales £1,000
IBM	USA	106,672
English Electric/Elliott	UK	89,515
*ICT	UK	75,830
Burroughs	USA	35,515
Honeywell	USA	19,577
Univac	USA	18,515
NCR	USA	18,360
Bull/GE	USA/France	7,355
CDC	USA	6,270
Ferranti	UK	3,379
GEC/AEI	UK	1,520
STC	USA	1,400
DEC	USA	1,385

*ICT, Plessey and English Electric now form International Computers Ltd in which the British government also has a holding.

The basic components of many British computers are also foreign, again largely American. Honeywell, for example, which has invested over £20 million in Britain, established a manufacturing organisation in Scotland some years ago and found that although they tried extremely hard to purchase components locally, the quality of British and European components was not suitable for their computers. Consequently a large percentage of the components themselves have to be imported from the USA. CDC also imports components and peripherals for all machines sold here.

IBM had the same problem both in the UK and Europe. In fact the IBM computers which are sold in the UK are assembled in France from discrete segments or sub-assemblies made in different parts of Europe. However, optical character recognition units are being made by IBM in Scotland for all worldwide marketing areas outside the USA and Canada.

Burroughs is building a new computer factory costing some £4 million in Glenrothes which will employ about 1,000. The new factory aims to be operational by 1970 and will turn out the complete range of computer products including central processors and peripheral equipment. The British company is the largest of the parent firm's overseas subsidiaries exporting some 75 per cent of its total production.

De La Rue Bull is the UK marketing subsidiary for the American General Electric Company's computers and has just concluded an arrangement with Systems Capital for financing the hire of computer facilities.

Control Data Corporation is a fast growing concern. Its parent company is in California and with its expansion into disc packs this company has joined Memorex, a British subsidiary of another Californian-based firm as the main rivals to IBM in the British market.

An Anglo-American partnership has been formed by the setting up of Indicon Automation which is owned jointly by the Reliance Gear Company of Huddersfield and the industrial electronics division of Thorn Bendix, itself owned by the Bendix Corporation of America and Thorn Electrical. Indicon will market a range of digital read-out equipment.

Electronic Associates of New Jersey is one of the best known manufacturers of analogue equipment in the world. Its British subsidiary is in Burgess Hill; the group also manufactures special purpose computing and electronic systems, precision electronic plotting equipment and laboratory instruments.

A sales and service organisation is being set up in London by Scientific Data Systems of California, makers of the Sigma range of computers. This move replaces a licensing arrangement by SDS in which GEC manufactured, sold and serviced SDS computers under a royalty agreement.

English Electric has an exchange of know-how with the American RCA as well as the German Siemens which latter company has frequently been quoted as a possible partner for the British International Computers complex. As indicated earlier in this section, Philips has entered the computer market in Europe manufacturing third generation machines.

Friden, the American company, has just entered the UK commercial computer terminal market, the firm is already well known for its electronic invoicing machines. A new British-based company, Racal-Milgo, has been formed to make and market data processing equipment as a result of an agreement between Racal Electronics of Bracknell and Milgo Electronic Corporation of Miami. Another joint venture, known as Mac-Attwood, has been formed by Adams-Millis and Attwood Electronics, to manufacture and sell magnetic computer tape and memory disc packs.

The Radio Corporation of America has 75 per cent of a company it has just set up in South Wales to manufacture tape and other magnetic products. Known as RCA Magnetic Products, International Computers owns the remaining quarter.

Audio Devices, the American computer and recording tape manufacturer, has set up Audev as its British marketing operation. The new company aims to get 25 per cent of the market, worth about £10 million a year and growing at some 20 per cent annually, within 18 months of becoming operational.

A new British company known as Calcomp has been formed by California Computer Products to market products and services. Its headquarters are at Kingston-on-Thames and the company will promote a full range of plotting systems and special application programme packages.

A major newcomer to computer leasing in the UK is Greyhound Equipment Finance, an off-shoot of the American Greyhound Group. The UK company is a wholly owned subsidiary of Greyhound's Swiss operation in which several international banks have an interest. These include Charterhouse; Japhet & Thomasson; the Ottoman Bank and Continental Illinois. Greyhound UK will invest some £15 million in financing capital equipment in other fields apart from computers. The group claims to be the world's largest owner/lessors of IBM equipment. Boothe Computer Corporation is another US leasing company which has set up an office in the UK.

Tally is the new name of the former Automatic Punched Tape, distributors of data processing peripherals and ancillaries. A British subsidiary of the Tally Corporation of Seattle, the company plans to manufacture in this country a large proportion of the products previously imported from its parent.

Leasco Data Processing Corporation, described as America's largest computer service organisation, has opened its European headquarters in London. The company is known as Leasco Europa. Computer Systems International, the software house, has a British branch and is also associated with Computerised Marketing Control Systems. Another computer services and programming house, Computer Services (Birmingham) is owned by University Computing Co of Dallas which is also parent to Benson-Lehner which makes plotters, coders, loggers, readers and the like.

Memory Magnetics, which has its manufacturing centre in California, currently imports its range of exchangeable disc packs for use in the magnetic disc stores of advanced computers. The company expects to manufacture in Britain shortly. Memory Magnetics is not alone in its drive on the UK disc pack market, estimated to be about £3 million annually. Scientific Furnishings, the Chichester firm, has been given exclusive rights to market disc packs by another Californian company, Caelus Memories of San Jose. Caelus itself has a cross-licensing agreement with IBM under which it employs the same oxide coating as in the latter's discs.

Other data processing equipment firms of American origin are Computer Sciences International, whose head office is in Los Angeles; Fabri Tek of Minneapolis which manufacturers memory systems; Anelex; Potter Instrument; Recognition Equipment and Mohawk Data Services.

One of the largest private programming schools of America, the Electronic Computer Programming Institute, which has 92 branches in the US, recently opened a British branch. It runs a 285 guinea, 300-hour course and has its own IBM machine to try out programmes.

IO
LEISURE ACTIVITIES

London's largest hotel at present is the American owned Hilton with 510 bedrooms. Trans World Airlines recently acquired control of Hilton's $44 million international operations. American investments in British hotels are heavy. The Hotel Corporation of America owns the Carlton Tower Hotel and is understood to be planning another large hotel in the London Airport vicinity. Knott Hotels operates through the Westbury Hotel in Bond Street. America's largest hotel-motel chain, Holiday Inns, which has almost 1,000 hotels in North America, Mexico and the Caribbean is making a major drive into Europe which includes plans for a $50 million investment in Britain. The company's aim is to build 10,000 hotel rooms here and immediate plans cover building three hotels, totalling 1,000 rooms, at Slough, Liverpool and London Airport. The company expects to have their hotels operational in 1971. BOAC and Intercontinental Hotels, a Pan American Airways subsidiary, are currently undertaking a joint project for a 1,000 bedroom hotel in the Victoria area.

Britain's biggest hotels group, Trust Houses, has a link with the Western International Hotels Company. Western, which is based in Seattle, operates 60 hotels in America and plans to make available all its resources for the promotion of Trust Houses hotels. In return a reservations office for Western will be opened in Grosvenor House. The arrangement has been cemented by a share exchange, 140,500 Trust Houses Ordinaries being exchanged for 10,000 shares of common stock in Western. Since this exchange Trust Houses and Western have become part of a consortium which has acquired stock of TraveLodge Corporation, the Santiago com-

68

pany which controls the second largest motel chain in America. Also included in the consortium is an Australian hotel concern.

Esso has entered the hotel business in Europe. Its largest hotel so far, at Maidenhead, has 100 bedrooms; it already owns an hotel in South Mimms and plans to build another in Edinburgh.

The French hotel company, Grands Hotels Réunies, also controls a New York organisation, Hotel Representatives Incorporated. HRI has a contracted membership of 83 European hotels including the Savoy group. London's Playboy club is American owned.

In the travel agency field the Swiss company Genossenschaft Hotelplan owns Inghams Travel and Hotel Plan. Tour Operators is financed by the American Express Company and National Cash Register. Bennett's the travel agency specialising in Scandinavian tours is Norwegian in origin. Club Mediterranée is a French holiday group controlled by Rothschild, the American Express recently took a 15 per cent stock interest in this concern.

Thoresen Car Ferries is Norwegian owned.

Samsonite, the luggage manufacturers is a Canadian Concern; A J Siris which also manufactures lightweight luggage is American.

Sports equipment shows further foreign investments. Nissen Trampoline, leading manufacturers of gymnastic apparatus, is American and its parent company is in Iowa; Pan Pacific is another US controlled manufacturer of sporting equipment and clothing. In golf and tennis equipment the leading name is the British Dunlop with its Slazenger subsidiary, but two American companies, Wilson Sporting Goods and A G Spalding & Brothers, also manufacture in the UK and each take some 5 per cent of the market in tennis balls and a somewhat higher share of the golf ball market. The Brunswick Corporation, active in sports equipment as well as surgical and laboratory instruments, is American owned. Uniroyal the American rubber concern has a golf ball manufacturing division.

The midlands-based Harris & Sheldon Group is to set up a glass fibre tube manufacturing plant in Alnwick as a result of a recently signed know-how agreement with Sportglass Incorporated of America. A subsidiary has been formed to manufacture and market the glass fibre tube which, in addition to providing blanks for a new range of Hardy fishing rods, will supply tubes for many industrial applications. Hardy's, a famous name in fishing tackle, belongs to the Harris & Sheldon Group. Another leading manufacturer of fishing tackle is Shakespeare & Co of Michigan through its British subsidiary Noris Shakespeare of Redditch which recently acquired Allcock, Lees & Youngs from Cope Allman.

H H Noble manufactures a range of trophies, cups and medals at its Belfast factory. It is a subsidiary of the Chicago company of the same name.

Kleinert Rubber, an American concern with a British associate, manufactures swimming caps as well as baby goods and a range of haberdashery products.

AMF International is the leading manufacturer of bowling alley equipment. It is a subsidiary of American Machine & Foundry of New York, employs 950 in Britain and has four subsidiaries over here. It also manufactures specialist engineering equipment such as water purification plant. An Australian owned company, Ainsworth Consolidated Industries, is active in the coin-operated dispensing and amusement equipment range. The Yorkshire-based Associated Pleasure Parks holds the franchise to operate Putt-Putt the American crazy-golf ranges.

Mattel of California claims to be the world's biggest toymaker. Its British subsidiary is Rosebud Mattel which is currently increasing its Rushden factory by 65,000 square feet and recruiting an extra 550 labour force. Rosebud plans to treble its £1·5 million a year turnover.

Dunbee-Combex has a link with Louis Marx of New York who invented the yo-yo and the instant insanity game. Aurora Plastics and Ohio Art both have fully owned British subsidiaries. Pallitoy, owned by Bakelite, produces such American toys as Action Man under licence. Impress International Merchandising has recently secured all UK licensing rights for Kwatro, a game that has swept the North American continent. Ideal Toy, another American company is active here, so is Bilo Toys which is Danish owned. Revell makes plastic construction toys and model kits and has its parent company based in California. Cosmic Crayon, the manufacturers of chalk, crayon and modelling materials, is owned by Binney & Smith of New York. Philips is joining forces with Mettoy to market its Philiform plastic constructional system. Philiform kits will be manufactured in the UK (previously they were imported from Holland) and distributed through Mettoy's nation-wide dealer network.

Denys Fisher, the toy manufacturing group, is making two products under licence from Kenner Toys, a General Foods subsidiary.

Family pets have come under American influence. The American Mars owns Thomas's, the Halifax group which makes Petcraft products, and also controls Walter Ellson reputed to be Britain's biggest pet accessories manufacturer and distributor.

Swiss watches have long been a popular luxury product. One of the largest Swiss companies is Omega which has a British subsidiary. America also has British investments in this area. Timex, a branch of the United States Time Corporation, has had a factory in Dundee since 1949. General Time of New York has been manufacturing from its Dumbarton factory since 1948. Other American watch and clock companies active in Britain are Bulova Watch Co, Elgin and Hamilton. Roamer, another popular make, is Swiss controlled. Luminising of clocks, watches, marine and aircraft instruments is carried out by Luminisers of Dumbarton, an associate of Luminous Processes of New York.

French jewellery interests are represented in Britain through Cartier, Boucheron and Chaumet. Kenwood Silver, the silversmiths, are American. In the sphere of costume jewellery Corocraft manufacturers and distributors of the Jewelcraft range is a subsidiary of Coro of New York. Sarah Coventry, another American range of costume jewellery, has just opened a factory in Scotland.

American owned firms account for around 40 per cent of pencils made in Britain. Familiar names include Eagle Pencil, Parker, Scripto and Venus. The most popular ball-point pen is Biro-BIC. The BIC empire was created by a Frenchman and the company makes nearly 5 million ball-points every day in factories throughout the world. In 1953 BIC bought Biro Swan and now has 55 per cent of the market. The next best selling ballpoint is Scripto which also sells under the trade name Scroll. Scripto Pens is a fully owned American subsidiary, its parent being in Atlanta. Venus Pen & Pencil has a New York head office and is also active in the ball point field. This company recently linked with the Esterbrook Pen Co whose British subsidiary Esterbrook Hazell is jointly owned by British Printing Corporation and the New Jersey-based Esterbrook. Esterbrook makes felt-tip pens under the brand names Gem, Relief and Flo-master. Gillette also makes ballpoints through its subsidiary Paper Mate which it acquired in 1955. Fountain pens again show strong American influence. Parker and Eversharp are both owned by Parker Pen of Wisconsin. Sheaffer is owned by Textron of Rhode Island; Valentine and Watermans are also American controlled.

Felt-tips is the province of Royal Sovereign which has the UK and European manufacturing rights of the Magic Marker Corporation of New York and also has an agreement with the Japan Stationery Company of Tokyo to market Pentel, the first fibre tip pen to be introduced into Britain four years ago. Magic Marker has a subsidiary in Beckenham which is responsible for a number of marking devices. Gillette's Paper Mate is about to launch a nylon-tip called Tempo.

Decca and EMI between them control more than 55 per cent of gramo-phone record sales in Britain; both are UK companies and distribute for a number of American labels. EMI handles Columbia, Parlophone, Tamla, Motown, Stateside, Dot, Bell, Waverley and Regal. The US company Audio Devices has just acquired Capitol Records, an EMI subsidiary, by issuing over three million shares in exchange for about 92 per cent of Capitol's outstanding shares held by EMI.

Decca also distributes for Deram and London. Music Corporation of America which previously sold its records in the UK through agents is about to begin trading in its own right. The associated labels of MCA are Unirecord, Decca USA, Brunswick, Coral, Vocalion and Review.

The Radio Corporation of America is planning a £1·5 million factory in Durham. Decca and RCA previously had an arrangement under which Decca manufactured and distributed the RCA/Victor label in this country. The RCA/Victor label, which the American company will now handle entirely in the UK, has between seven and ten per cent of the market.

CBS is a subsidiary of the Columbia Broadcasting System which produces gramophone records under its own label and also owns Oriole records. The Dutch Philips, under its own label and that of Fontana, sells well in Britain as does Deutsche Grammophon and its subsidiary Polydor. DGG is part German as it is owned jointly by Siemens and Philips. Philips has further strengthened its interests in Britain's entertainments industry by its purchase of Chappell & Company, the Bond Street music shop and theatre ticket agency. Management of the Chappell companies (there is a New York Office) is to be shared by North American Philips, NV Philips and Siemens. The MGM agreement with EMI under which the British company holds both licensing and distribution rights is currently being disputed by Pye Records.

Supraphon, a range of low-price high quality classical recordings distributed through bookshops, department stores and stationers, is Czechoslovakian. M A Millar, makers of sapphire needles, is American with headquarters in Illinois. The company has a factory in County Down.

The American owned Steinway puts grand pianos in almost all British and overseas concert halls. Rippen Piano Factories, which make Lindner pianos, is Dutch owned. In 1967 Rippen sold 1,356 pianos in Britain, representing over 15 per cent of total retail sales. Hammond Organ which makes both organs and pianos is jointly owned by Boosey & Hawkes and the Hammond Corporation of Chicago. Herrburger-Brooks which makes piano actions, piano keys and the like was founded in 1810; it is 45 per cent owned by the Jasper Corporation of Indiana. Baldwin-Burns, suppliers of guitars, amplifiers and organs is a subsidiary of D H Baldwin of America; Wurlitzer has a sales agent in Britain and also uses Ditchburn as its distributor.

Two major artists agencies operating in this country are both American controlled. These are General Artists Corporation, whose British subsidiary is G A C Redway and Creative Management Associated.

It has been estimated that more than 80 per cent of films made in Great Britain are financed by American capital. All the major US film companies operate or distribute here including Twentieth Century-Fox and its subsidiary British Movietonews; Columbia Pictures (in which the Banque de Paris has a 20 per cent stake) and its subsidiary Screen Gems; RKO; Metro-Goldwyn-Mayer; Walt Disney Productions and United Artists which is owned by the Transamerica Corporation. Associated British Picture Corporation's UK subsidiary Associated British-Pathe also distributes for the Columbia Broadcasting System; Warner Brothers has a British subisidiary, so does Paramount which is now part of Gulf & Western Industries.

The Music Corporation of America films in Britain and planned to spend some £10 million during 1968 making eight pictures. The British owned film companies such as Rank and ABC are frequently involved in co-productions with companies such as Columbia, United Artists and Paramount.

The Commonwealth United Corporation, a US company, is expanding its activities in Europe by setting up two UK film production and distribution companies which also aims to acquire cinemas and property in this country.

Ninety per cent of cinematic film and two-fifths of roll film are produced by Kodak, a subsidiary of the America Eastman Kodak. Kodak started its British operations in 1898. Three per cent of its net sales are paid to the parent company as royalties.

In colour photography Kodak again has well over 60 per cent of the market. Ilford which is owned 40 per cent by the Swiss CIBA and 60 per cent by ICI has some 15 per cent of the UK market. Agfa-Gevaert which is a Belgium-German combination has an eight per cent share. Also popular is Ferranis of Italy which is owned by the Minnesota Mining & Manufacturing Company and the Swiss Bolex. Most of the photographic film base in this country is made by Bexford which is jointly owned by Bakelite Xylonite and Ilford. Anscochrome colour transparency films are now on sale in the UK. They are produced by General Aniline & Film whose British operation is based on new London premises which include a processing laboratory.

Technicolor is an American cine process whose British distributor is the Rank Organisation. Westrex which makes projectors, sound recording and similar equipment is American, so is the Minneapolis-based Pako and Pavelle of New York, both make printing and processing equipment for photographic and graphic arts interests.

There are more than 1,000 different models of still cameras and some 440 types of movie cameras available for the photographer, amateur or professional. Kodak is the brand leader and other major manufacturers are Ilford; Bell & Howell; Agfa-Gevaert and the Japanese Yashica. Other imported makes include the German Leica and Rolleiflex and the Swedish Hasselblad. Polaroid, which makes photographic products, film and lenses, operates under licence from the American company of the same name.

A number of Eastern European exporters have looked to British firms for their UK distribution, marketing and know-how and have set up joint ventures and instigated licensing arrangements. Technical & Optical Equipment, which has the exclusive UK distribution for a range of Russian equipment including cameras, film and optic, has in fact been acquired by its Russian partners; the company is now owned by the Russian Mashpriborintorg (90 per cent) and the Moscow Narodny Bank (10 per cent). Technical & Optical Equipment plans to double its size and is expected to launch a new line of Russian transistor radios.

II

CONSTRUCTION AND CIVIL ENGINEERING

Alcan, British Aluminium, Booth and Imperial Aluminium account for 73 per cent or more of Britain's aluminium semi-manufactures market. Alcan is Canadian owned; British Aluminium is owned by Tube Investments (49 per cent) and Reynolds Metals of America (51 per cent). Imperial Aluminium is 75 per cent owned by the Aluminium Company of Chicago. James Booth Aluminium is a joint subsidiary of Alcan and Kaiser Aluminium of California. Wickeder Eisen und Stahlwerk the large German company is setting up a £300,000 plant in St Helens to make aluminium-coated steel. Hunter Aluminium of Aston Clinton, makers of aluminium sheeting is a subsidiary of American Metal Climax of New York, so too is MacKamax Aluminium which manufactures aluminium architectural and other extruded sections at its Staffordshire factory.

Float, fibre and optical glass is dominated by Pilkingtons. Pilkington Perkin-Elmer was formed in 1966 to utilise the resources of the British company with the know-how of America's Perkin-Elmer Corporation. This company operates from a factory in North Wales and has a near monopoly of flat glass in the UK. Pilkington has also expressed an interest in the possibility of making Owens-Illinois Cer-Vit in this country. Cer-Vit is a substance which has all the desirable properties of glass with the added attraction of being resistant to thermal shock of sudden temperature changes, abrasion and chemical attack.

British Paints is owned by the Celanese Corporation of America; Griffiths Bros, another leading paint manufacturer, is owned by the US Interchemical Corporation. These, together with ICI, account for about half the British paint market. Enfield Chemicals, also paint manufacturers, is owned by the Flintkote Company of New York. Similarly Sterling Varnish has an American parent; Ripolin is French owned. Dupli-Colour, the touch-up aerosol paints, is marketed under licence by the Cope Allman subsidiary, Lloyds Industries.

Carson-Paripan has an agreement with the Valspar Corporation of America covering a complete exchange of technical and marketing know-how. Carson-Paripan first developed the spectromatic colour-matching system under licence from an American company some years ago. Incidentally the US company has no connection with the Valspar paints which are made by Goodlass Wall in the UK.

Sixty per cent of boilers installed in British buildings are made by American owned companies, the main suppliers being Ideal-Standard, Crane and Florence Stoves. Ideal is owned by American Standard of New York and it controls a number of UK subsidiaries making bathroom and heating equipment. Crane has a large factory in Aycliffe and is itself parent to a number of subsidiary interests in the UK.

Aladdin Industries associated with the American Aladdin makes a number of heating appliances and lamps. Bahco-Condrup, Swedish owned, is well known for heating equipment and such appliances as primus stoves. Alfa-Laval, also Swedish, makes centrifugal pumps, heat exchange systems and heating equipment. Carpenter & Paterson, manufacturers of central heating equipment, has an American parent. This company is currently expanding its Welsh premises.

The swing from central heating to air conditioning is becoming an important aspect of the building industry. The Electricity Council is actively trying to promote the £15 million a year market for air conditioning. Rootes Tempair has well over half the market, Rootes being part of Chrysler as mentioned in the section on the motor industry. The world's leading air conditioning manufacturers is the Carrier Corporation of New York whose British subsidiary, Carlyle Air Conditioning, claims some 35-40 per cent of the market. Lennox Industries of Iowa has just entered the British air conditioning market although the company is already an important manufacturer of warm-air heating systems through its Croydon subsidiary. A British challenger in air conditioning equipment, Normalair-Garrett, is 48 per cent American owned by the Garrett Corporation of Los Angeles. Normalair, which also makes aircraft pressurisation and oxygen breathing equipment recently won a Queen's award for export achievement. The How Group of Companies, Staffordshire based, is in partnership with the Swedish firm Luftkonditionering. Trane, whose parent is in Wisconsin has a factory in Fife, the company makes air conditioning, heating and ventilating equipment.

Industrial resins and adhesives are made by Bostik which is a subsidiary of the American United Shoe Machinery Corporation. Bostik makes a range of sealing and coating compounds for both building industry and do-it-yourself experts. National Adhesives & Resins, owned by National Starch & Chemical of New York, and Leicester Lovell, Canadian owned, are both major manufacturers of adhesives. Also active is the Swiss CIBA with its Aerodux, Aerolite, Araldite, Ardux and Melolam products.

Dow Corning's Silastic, the American made silicone rubber sealant, is distributed in this country by Midland Silicones.

Formica, which maintains about half the market for decorative laminates was first made by Formica Insulation of Cincinatti, De La Rue acquiring the Formica rights in 1946. Today Formica International which is registered in London is 40 per cent owned by the American Cyanamid Company and the remainder by De La Rue. Warerite is the second most popular laminate with about a fifth of the market. Warerite is made by Bakelite which also manufactures a range of laminates and household plastic articles, Bakelite being a subsidiary of Bakelite-Xylonite which is jointly owned by Distillers and Union Carbide. Another popular laminate, Arborite, is owned by the Canadian Dominion Tar & Chemical Company. Arborite has about a sixth of the market and recently took over the production of Fablon. Imported laminates form a small share of the market, the Swedish Perstrop being one of the most popular of these. Monsanto also owns a number of subsidiaries in the household and building plastic spheres. Pirelli, the Italian group, aims to capture a major share of the British plastic laminates market and is currently launching a 36-colour range of laminates made in Turin.

Lafarge Aluminous Cement is French owned. Terrapin which makes and assembles a range of prefabricated buildings, imports from Danish Reszka; Butler Buildings manufactures steel buildings at its Coventry works; its parent company is in Kansas City.

Vickers is joining forces with Wedag of Western Germany in the manufacture of cement plants. A joint company has been set up in Germany with Wedag holding 60 per cent, another will be operated in Britain with Vickers having a 51 per cent interest.

The construction industry shows a number of licensing arrangements. For example Robert Douglas, the building and civil engineering contractors, hold the licence for an American reinforced concrete building system called Lift-Slab which can be used for car parks or office buildings and flats. A subsidiary of J L Keir, another large firm of contractors, holds the licence from a Finnish company to produce Isocrete, a lightweight aerated concrete with high insulation properties.

Taylor Woodrow manufactures an industrialised housing system under licence from the Danish firm of Larsen & Nielsen.

Tracoba, one of the Gilbert-Ash industrialised building systems which is used for blocks of flats, is French in origin.

John Laing, the second largest construction company in Britain, has the UK licence from a Danish contractor to manufacture a heavy concrete panel system used for building large blocks of flats. Laing's has three factories manufacturing components for this system.

The French industralised building system Camus owns half of Camus Great Britain and sub-licenses to three British companies. In effect Camus sells its know-how and derives its profits from royalties made on its contracts. In mid-1968 Fram Higgs & Hill (Camus) opened its third UK factory.

An agreement has just been completed between Inn Keepers Supply (a subsidiary of Holiday Inns of Memphis) and GUS Export International for the exchange of know-how and experience in equipping hotels, universities, schools and hospitals. The manufacturing resources of both companies will co-operate and will exchange designs and features for manufacture on both sides of the Atlantic.

The Dutch firm Hulo is building a brick handling equipment plant on Tees-side; Anglo-Dutch interests are further represented by Truscon, an important building and civil engineering contractor which makes concrete extrusions and precast flooring units. A substantial minority of Truscon's shares is owned by Shell.

BPB Industries is the dominant producer of plaster and plasterboard in the UK with 80 per cent of the market. Some 14·9 per cent of the equity of BPB is owned by United States Gypsum Company, the largest gypsum mining group in the world, which nominates two directors to the BPB board. British Plaster Board has a subsidiary company which manufactures roofing felt, damp proof courses and other building material and engineering products.

The German Thyssen has a British subsidiary and through this controls a number of companies offering services and materials to the construction industries.

Stonhard-Tremco, building maintenance materials manufacturers, is jointly owned by Tremco Manufacturing of Cleveland and the British firm Berger Jenson & Nicholson. Bitumin Industries which manufactures both bituminous and non-bituminous compounds under the trade names Colset, Solbit and Embit is another subsidiary of the United Shoe Machinery Corporation. Grahams (Seacroft) a subsidiary of Schlegel Manufacturing makes narrow fabrics for the building industry and textile trades.

Cape Asbestos has a subsidiary, Marinite, owned jointly with the Johns-Manville Corporation of America, which makes fireproof panels for marine and land use. Marinite has a factory in Glasgow.

Morganite Ceramic Fibres, which manufactures Kaowool heat insulating ceramic, is owned 60 per cent by Morgan Crucible of London and 40 per cent by Babcock & Wilcox of New York. The British Babcock & Wilcox has an arrangement with its American counterpart which gives it access to US techniques particularly in the field or refractory and nuclear power plant construction; it also manufactures excavators under licence.

Celotex is a market leader for insulating materials, fibre building boards, tiles and the like. The company has its parent located in Florida and currently imports most of its materials into the UK.

Tarmac, the largest producer of road making materials in the UK, has a 50 per cent interest in a bitumen refinery with Phillips Petroleum of America.

Spaulding Fibre has held a five per cent share in the UK company of the same name since 1907. In 1961 it bought out the British holding.

Spaulding manufactures insulation materials, vulcanised fibre and laminated plastics. American interests penetrate further sections of the building materials industry through H H Robertson, which makes roofing, flooring and ventilation equipment and Schacht Associates which is active in stainless steel architectural metalwork.

Uniroyal, the subsidiary of the American company of the same name, manufactures rubber products including flooring. Armstrong Cork is a leading manufacturer of household flooring compounds, acoustic materials, rubber and industrial adhesives. The company has a large factory in Gateshead and a Pennsylvania-based parent. Amtico Flooring which manufactures vinyl floor tiles in Coventry is jointly owned by American Biltrite Rubber and British Celanese.

Luxaflex, makers of venetian blinds, is owned by Hunter Douglas International of New York; fire protection equipment manufacturer Walter Kidde is another American company active in Britain. Industrial silencing equipment is made by Industrial Acoustics which is associated with the New York company of the same name. Rentokil, the pest control experts, has the majority of its shares held by the Danish A S Sophus Berendsen. Cobra (Wood Treatment) is American owned. Yale Locks is part of Eaton Yale & Towne, the large American group active in a range of products including builders' hardware. Otis Elevator, one of the largest American manufacturers of lifts and escalators, has nearly 40 per cent of the British market. The company employs 3,000 in the UK. Hammond & Champness, an old established British firm of lift makers which has taken over three smaller manufacturers has an association with the Dover Corporation of New York covering technical know-how.

Sanitary fittings are made by Nibco, an American company with a Dundee factory.

Earthmoving equipment and building trucks have already been mentioned in the chapter on the motor industry where we have seen that Caterpillar Tractor and Euclid, the two American owned companies, are market leaders. Another active manufacturer of materials handling equipment is Eaton Yale & Towne which specialises in fork-lift trucks, its British subsidiary being in Wednesfield. Rack Engineering is an American subsidiary and Ruston-Bucyrus is jointly owned by Bucyrus-Erie of Wisconsin and Ruston & Hornsby; both manufacture materials handling and excavating equipment in the UK.

John Wallace Mechanical Handling is licensed by the Bulgarian Balkancar to assemble fork-lift trucks in its Glasgow factory. Balkancar is reputed to be Europe's largest manufacturer of fork-lift trucks and the products are marketed in Britain under the name Wallace-Rila.

Semi-trailer suppliers Crane Freuhauf is one-third owned by the American Freuhauf Company.

Arrow Construction Equipment whose parent company is in Denver, is known for civil engineering plant and road trailers; in the same sphere of operations is Barber-Greene Olding owned by Barber-Greene of Illinois.

Wheway Watson, makers of chains, lifting and mechanical handling equipment is financially associated with Columbus-McKinnon Corporation. British Jeffrey-Diamond is a subsidiary of Jeffrey Galion Manufacturing Company of Ohio and is well-known for self-loading dumpers and a range of mining equipment. J I Case Company, with a Wisconsin-based parent, makes earthmoving equipment together with a number of basic models for industrial and constructional use including crawler and wheeled tractors, harvesters and the like.

Clark Equipment, a wholly-owned subsidiary of the Michigan company of the same name, produces a wide range of earthmoving equipment, fork-lift trucks and the like. The company is a large exporter.

Orenstein & Koppel, a leading German manufacturer of excavators and constructors' plant is currently discussing with National Carbonising the setting up of a joint subsidiary to sell direct to the UK market. Crown Controls Corporation of Ohio has introduced a new fork-lift truck into this country.

Tirfor is a subsidiary of the French Tractel and makes a range of hand-operated lifting and pulling machines, hydraulic fork and trolley lifts, travel jacks, scaffolding winches and the like. The Norwegian firm Sverre Munck makes cranes of all sizes at its Hebburn works. Construction Equipment & Machinery, a subsidiary of Clipper Manufacturing of Kansas City, makes masonry and concrete saws and core drills. Germany's Demag, already established in the UK as a supplier of German-built equipment and heavy machinery for the chemical and petrochemical industry, is setting up a manufacturing plant in Oxfordshire for hoists, cranes and engineering equipment generally. The company is one of the world's largest manufacturers of engineering equipment.

Wire ropes, clips and fittings are made by Crosby-Laughlin a subsidiary of American Hoist & Derrick Company.

Ransomes & Rapier is a subsidiary of the British-owned Newton Chambers. Koehring Company of America has some 40 per cent of the shares of Ransomes & Rapier which manufactures a range of mobile cranes, hydraulically operated earthmoving equipment and hydraulic and mechanical powered truck mixers.

Recently the two largest British groups in the compressed air industry – Broom & Wade and Holman merged into a £28 million combine. Their main competitors are the Swedish Atlas Copco, active in drilling equipment and hand tools, and the US Ingersoll-Rand group which also makes a range of mining and construction equipment, electric tools and the like. Nordberg Manufacturing, whose head office is in Milwaukee, is also active in the manufacture of compressors and hoists together with rock ore crushers and equipment for railroad maintenance. Boyle Bros Drilling, a Canadian owned company, manufactures rotary drilling machines and another American company, Arrow Construction Equipment, makes civil engineering plant and road trailers at its Blyth works. Parsons Chain, a subsidiary of American Chain & Cable, manufactures a wide range of chain, suspension gear and attachments for mechanical handling.

Domestic power tools is dominated by Black & Decker which is American owned and claims almost 90 per cent of the home market together with 85 per cent of the £5·6 million export market. Black & Decker, whose parent is in Maryland, has been in operation since 1925 and has a labour force of 2,000. Its competitors are US owned Stanley-Bridges and Wolf in which North American Rockwell has an 18 per cent stake.

The leading manufacturer of refuse incinerators is Motherwell Bridge-Tacol which makes a rolling grate incinerator under licence from Vereinigte Kesselwerke of Düsseldorf. Heenan & Froude markets an American designed machine, the Heenan Nichols continuous incinerator; Head Wrightson manufacturers, again under licence, a machine designed by Josef Martin of Munich.

Two of Europe's leading manufacturers of hydro-electric plant now collaborate in the design, manufacture and sale of pump and water turbines for hydro-electric power schemes throughout the world. The companies are English Electric and Escher Wyss of Zurich which already collaborates closely with Sulzer Brothers of Winterthur and has acquired the latter's storage pump business. English Electric and Sulzer, whose interests in hydraulic equipment is also world-wide, have themselves been associated in the design and manufacture of pump turbines since 1960. In future English Electric/Escher Wyss will put forward joint proposals for the development of the pumped storage and hydro-electric projects now being studied in different parts of the world.

ADVERTISING, MARKETING, PUBLIC RELATIONS
RESEARCH AND CONSULTANCY

A glance down the list of Britain's top ten advertising agencies will show all but two (Masius Wynne-Williams and London Press Exchange) to be fully-owned subsidiaries or, in the case of S H Benson, with an overseas agency taking a minority interest. Lintas, one of the top ten, is somewhat in a class of its own as it is owned by the Anglo-Dutch Unilever and is virtually financed by the British end of that operation.

As would be expected American investment in advertising agencies is strong. Wholly-owned American agencies active in this country are J Walter Thompson the biggest of them all, the Interpublic Group (McCann-Erickson; Erwin Wasey; Quadrant; Pritchard Wood) and BBDO the agency which handles the Republican Party advertising in the USA.

Benton & Bowles; Norman, Craig & Kummel (which bought Crane Advertising), Foote, Cone & Belding; and Grant are familiar names in the agency world as is Ted Bates, which bought John Hobson's agency in 1959 and started the post-war American penetration into the British agency scene.

In the case of Ogilvy & Mather, a certain amount of cross fertilisation has taken place here as David Ogilvy, an Englishman, formed his own agency in New York with the financial assistance of two British agencies, the then Mather & Crowther and S H Benson. Child took over parent shortly after the agreement with Bensons was terminated in 1963 when Mather & Crowther changed its name to Ogilvy & Mather to become a subsidiary of the US agency.

Continuing through the list of American-owned agencies we find Papert Koenig Lois; Young & Rubicam; Burnett-Nicholson (a subsidiary of Leo Burnett which bought Leggett Nicholson), Geer, DuBois; Doyle, Dane, Bernbach; Charles Hobson & Grey (the British Charles Hobson being bought by the New York agency) and we are told to stand by for another American take-over when one of the most spectacular of recent Madison Avenue successes Wells, Rich, Greene links up with a British agency. America is not the only country with advertising agencies and capital to invest overseas. London has two French owned agencies – Havas and Publicis; a South African – Lindsay Smithers; two Australians: Jackson Wain and Ayer, and the Canadian Maclaren which bought Dunkley & Friedlander, now Maclaren, Dunkley Friedlander. Another recent arrival is Marsteller which has a Jermyn Street office. Until a short while ago this agency operated through a public relations outlet – cs Services-Burson-Marsteller which also occupies the new offices.

Masius International, the overseas company of Masius, Wynne-Williams has reversed the trend by buying an American agency, Street & Finney.

A number of agencies have set up joint ventures with American agencies, among them Charles Vernon with D'Arcy and an increasing number of British agencies have Americans holding minority shares. These include Garland-Compton; Butler & Gardner; Colman Prentis & Varley (with Kenyon & Eckhardt), Lennen & Newell; Sharp, McManus; S H Benson (with Needham, Harper & Steers having a 20 per cent voting interest); Brunning (with Post-Keys Gardner); Freeman, Mathes & Milne (Canadian-financed); and Roles & Parker which is also partly financed by Marsteller.

One of the biggest market research companies is A C Nielsen. Its Oxford offices employs 800 and it is a fully-owned subsidiary of the Chicago parent. J Walter Thompson's British Market Research Bureau is another active firm of researchers; Gallup, of political poll fame, is also American owned, and Marplan is part of the Interpublic group. Roger Williams Technical & Economic Services, the New Jersey company which specialises in market research for the chemical industries, has a London office. Audience Studies, the company which pre-tests television commercials, is owned by the Columbia Pictures Corporation.

Recently introduced into the UK is equipment known as the Votometer which is used in market research to record audience reaction. This is American in origin and is marketed by Votometer (Great Britain).

Also new to this country is Photomotion, a Canadian system of animated back projection, used for sales meetings, advertising presentations and the like.

Infoplan, part of the Interpublic group is one of the largest public relations consultancies in Britain. Brook-Hart, Ruder & Finn is a subsidiary of the New York pr concern Ruder & Finn. Bureau of Commercial Information is another Interpublic subsidiary specialising in public relations and Daniel J Edelman has also set up an office in London. This is one of the 'big five' American public relations companies. Carl Byoir, yet another New York pr firm, has a London office in Berkeley Square.

Reputedly the world's biggest show business pr agency, Rogers, Cowan & Brenner of New York and Los Angeles now has a London office.

British publishers generally prepare their own advertising, a peculiarly English habit which an American firm, Denhard & Stewart has counter-attacked by starting a UK branch. This New York company specialises in book advertising.

The American direct selling agency Wunderman, Ricotta & Kline has linked up with the Lonsdale Hands Organisation to form a British end to the business known as Lonsdale-Wunderman Direct Marketing. The company currently bills $25 million in the USA.

One of the largest contract selling organisations, which supplies sales force on a temporary basis, is Merchandising Manpower, a Young & Rubicam subsidiary. Salespower, a subsidiary of Manpower, another US firm, also provides temporary help in this area of selling.

United Premium Advertising, one of the leading firms specialising in this form of promotion, is American.

E F MacDonald International, the Ohio-based sales incentive company, has a London office. A new agency called Underline formed to offer expertise in all the 'below the line' sides of marketing (premium offers and the like) has Foote Cone & Belding as its major shareholder with a 52 per cent shareholding. Another partner in this company is Abbey Goodman, owned by Ilford.

Walt Disney's merchandising division brings the parent company 13 million dollars annually in licensing fees from outlets round the world. The British side of the operation makes a contribution by means of large scale Mickey Mouse, Donald Duck and Pluto promotions as well as the sales of books and gramophone records.

Eyeline Films, which produce screen and television commercials, has an exclusive agreement with Cine Eddizioni Pubblicita of Rome for a two-way association of talent, productions and experience.

Another form of promotion is trading stamps and here one of the largest operators are the US company Sperry & Hutchinson which is also currently test marketing in Britain for Sunset House, an American mail order company having an £8 million turnover, with a view to setting up a British organisation for the latter. Sperry & Hutchinson is itself diversifying, the parent company recently acquired Bigelow-Sanford one of the largest carpet companies in the USA. The British licensees are Kosset Carpets and the Carpet Manufacturing Company. Sperry & Hutchinson has just built a large merchandise distribution centre at Manchester and has also taken over Western Girl, the employment office specialising in temporary help.

The oldest and largest foreign owned chain store is Woolworths which is American controlled and has some 1,100 freehold and leasehold retail stores in the British Isles. Some 52·7 per cent of its ordinary stock is owned by F W Woolworth Co, USA. The Safeway chain of supermarkets is American owned and the Regent Street store Galeries LaFayette is a subsidiary of the French department store of the same name.

Bulman Store Equipment which manufactures display fixtures is American, and Abbey Goodman a leading designer and manufacturer of display equipment and publicity material is owned by Ilford, which is itself 40 per cent owned by the Swiss CIBA. C & A is a privately owned business belonging to the Dutch Brenninkmeyer family since 1841.

Visnews, the international newsfilm agency is a non-profit making organisation jointly owned by the BBC, Reuters, the Rank Organisation, the Australian Broadcasting Commission, and the Broadcasting Corporations of Canada and New Zealand. Reuters itself is controlled by interests representing British, Australian and New Zealand newspapers.

The Wells Organisation is the largest firm of fund raisers of their kind and this company is American in origin.

In the field of consultancy and research both Battelle and Arthur D Little are fully-owned American subsidiaries. The Metra Consulting Group is French owned, some of its finance being supplied by the Banque de Paris. Booz-Allen & Hamilton, the biggest management consultancy fiom in the world which has had an office in London for some years, took vrer the British operational research experts BOR in April 1968.

McKinsey, another large American-based firm of consultants, has been retained by the BBC and British Railways. Webb Associates, the US ergonomics consultancy, has extended its services to Britain by forming Webb Associates (International) with the British industrial design company Eric Marshall Associates. Two other American owned management consultancy firms active in Britain are Stevenson, Jordan & Harrison and Graham Parker, which specialises in industrial and technical consultancy.

Stanford Research Institute of California is planning to open an economic, market and physical science division in the UK. The Boston Consulting Group has formed a joint venture with the Attwood Group to specialise in company strategy formation, the company is called Attwood Boston Consultants. Knight Wegenstein, the Swiss-based management consultancy, also recently opened a London office.

Urwick Diebold, an Urwick Orr subsidiary, is closely associated with the Diebold Group of New York. This concern offers management training courses and computer consultancy services.

Louis A Allen Associates, whose headquarters is in California, now has a UK subsidiary in Guildford. This company plans and runs management seminars for industry. Industrial Education International, which is also a specialist organisation concerned with management seminars, is an American company with a London office.

Success Motivation, a managerial training course system, and the Dale Carnegie courses for salesmen are both American-originated franchise operations.

Intertext Training Services is a subsidiary (through the Intertext Group) of International Correspondence Schools of America. This new subsidiary is hoping to enter the UK training market through offering 'tutorial workshops' on the principle of taking the training course to employees instead of sending staff on external courses.

Berlitz Schools, well known for language tuition, is French in origin. The language laboratory is an American invention, so is the quicker reading course, an example of which, the Evelyn Wood Rapid Reading Institute, has opened in London. This concern is owned by Famous Artists.

Willy Scheidegger, the Swiss Typewriting School, now has a UK operation located in Wembley.

Personnel and management selection consultants Hay-MSL is the result of a joint venture between the British MSL Group and the Philadelphian Edward N Hay. Personnel Evaluation & Research, another firm of management selection experts and industrial psychologists is a subsidiary of Marketing Survey & Research Corporation of New York. Heidrick & Struggles, one of America's older executive selection companies has just opened a London office.

Randstad, a Dutch employment agency which has been operating on a small scale in Britain for the past year, has just started a big drive for more UK business. Its headquarters are in Victoria Street with two branch offices; it aims to have a chain of 45.

Manpower, the £70 million a year supplier of contract labour operating in 500 cities throughout the world is American owned. Many of its offices are operated through franchise agreements.

13

ELECTRONICS, TELECOMMUNICATIONS AND DEFENCE

Companies most active in the field of electrical and electronic equipment

Company	where based
Plessey	*UK*
GEC/AEI	*UK*
Philips	*Netherlands*
RCA	*USA*
General Electric Company of America	*USA*
English Electric/Elliott	*UK*
Westinghouse	*USA*
Perkin-Elmer	*USA*

These are not listed in order of size; the electronics industry is so diverse that the companies involved are to be found in the field of household appliances, office equipment, scientific instruments and as many other spheres as there is a need for electronic components.

The home-grown industry benefits from American knowledge and licences to a very large extent.

According to Basil de Ferranti, 37 per cent of integrated circuits sold in Britain are wholly imported from the us and another 19 per cent are imported in a partly finished condition for assembly here.

The American owned Texas Instruments claims almost 40 per cent of the market estimated to be running at over £16 million a year. Texas is also the source, direct or indirect, of most of the TTL (translator-transistor logic) devices sold in Britain, and the company pays licence fees to its parent.

Its main rival in microelectronics is SGS-Fairchild which has a 30 per cent market share and has just opened a microcircuit diffusion facility at its Falkirk factory.

SGS-Fairchild is an interesting example of international investment. The Planer process for producing semiconductors was developed some ten years ago at the research laboratories of the Fairchild Camera & Instrument Corporation of America. After setting up manufacturing facilities in the USA, Fairchild examined the various ways they could exploit their invention in Europe. In 1961 the company acquired a one-third interest in Societa Generale Semiconduttor Spa of Italy. Up to that time SGS had produced germanium transistors for use in the equipment of its owners which were two Italian companies – Olivetti and Telettra, together with the General Electric Company of America. Fairchild acquired General Electric's interest and provided the new affiliate, now called SGS-Fairchild, with the know-how to manufacture and market silicon Planar semiconductors throughout Europe, the Middle East and Africa. The company created a series of marketing teams in the main Western European countries and in 1962 SGS-Fairchild was formed in the UK. Today the company operates as an autonomous unit but works in close co-operation with the other companies within the group. As we go to press it is learned that Olivetti has bought Fairchild's one-third interest in SGS-Fairchild. Through a separate transaction the exchange of technical know-how between Fairchild and SGS and patent cross-licenses are continued on a non-exclusive basis.

The only wholly-owned British companies possessing large scale capabilities for the manufacture of semiconductor integrated circuits are Elliott, Ferranti, Marconi and Plessey. Marconi and Elliott have recently joined forces in their microcircuit interests. All these manufacturers have licensing agreements with various American companies.

Mullard, a Philips subsidiary, is investing £15 million over the next four years in the Associated Semiconductor venture it owns with GEC primarily to make microcircuits. Plessey and the American Philco-Ford have also set up a joint venture to make semiconductor devices, transistors and integrated circuits. The new company acts as licensee for General Instruments Corporation of New Jersey. General Instruments itself has a British subsidiary active in semiconductors, as does Transitron Electronic of Massachusetts another important American company with an expanding production facility in Maidenhead.

Thorn Electrical Industries recently signed a 12-year agreement with International Rectifier of California, under which the American concern will provide technical assistance and licences relating to semiconductor products and will receive a management fee in return. International Rectifier already has a British subsidiary located in Oxted which supplies electrical and photoelectric equipment. Under the new arrangement

Thorn will have a say in the operation of IR's European subsidiaries with the American company exercising management control.

Although the General Post Office has announced the disbandment of the bulk supply agreement on telephone apparatus made by GEC-AEI, Plessey and Standard Telephones & Cables, the terms of the pact have been extended until April 1971. Plessey and GEC-AEI have 40 per cent each of the market for telephone exchange equipment, STC has 20 per cent. After 1971 the chief firms which will benefit will be British Insulated Callender's Cables; Automatic Telephone; Ericsson Telephone; Marconi; Phoenix and Telephone Rentals as well as the three companies which already participate. Automatic Telephone and Ericsson are both Plessey subsidiaries. Ericsson is not to be confused with the Swedish concern of that name.

Standard Telephones & Cables claims 50 per cent of the world market for submarine cables. The company is owned by ITT, although its parent has little or no say in the British activities and only one American figures among the 350 people who make up its executive management. The company's turnover runs at about £100 million. It employs nearly 32,000 and exports 40 per cent of its output which covers a wider across-the-board range of telecommunications and electronic products than any other British company, although telephone exchanges and cables account for the majority of its activities. The British Broadcasting Corporation recently placed an order worth some £200,000 with STC for a computer-controlled automatic data exchange.

Another active cable and telecommunications equipment manufacturer is Sterling Cable, a subsidiary of A C Cossor which is owned by the Raytheon Company of Massachusetts. Plessey is the major home contender in the telecommunications industry with 40 per cent of the UK market.

The Swedish Ericsson Company has formed a new British company aimed at capturing a large part of post office communications equipment buying. Ericsson's net sales are £185 million plus.

Guest Electronics which acts as distributor for Yugoslavia's Iskra electronic components aims at a £6 million plus share of the electronic components market for this concern. Guest also distributes electronic components for Tekelec-Airtronic of France and SP Electronic of Italy.

Emerson & Cuming, a US concern, has established a British manufacturing facility for dielectric and microwave equipment. Another American company, C P Clare, which manufactures mercury-wetted contact and reed relays, switchlights and gang-switch assemblies, has commenced production in its Watford factory. Semiconductor Specialists of Chicago has formed a sales and stocking facility in West Drayton. The company distributes solid-state products and the British centre offers equipment manufactured by Fairchild, Motorola, RCA, Westinghouse, Signetic, ITT, Siliconix, General Electric, Clevite Piezoelectric, Augat and other familiar US products.

The aircraft industry shows much foreign investment, thanks in part to the number of licensing agreements between British aircraft manufacturers and the large amount of overseas capital invested in aircraft components. Concorde itself is the result of Anglo-French co-operation; British, French and West German interests are currently developing the European air-bus although the future of this project is in some doubt due to economic pressures. If it falls through, three leading American companies, Lockheed, McDonnell Douglas and Boeing are all standing by with 300-seater versions. McDonnell Douglas has a licensing arrangement with Short Brothers & Harland for which the US Rohr is currently bidding.

Bristol Aerojet, the leading aircraft equipment manufacturer is half owned by Aerojet-General of California and half by Rolls-Royce through the latter's ownership of Bristol Aircraft. As well as aircraft equipment and components Bristol makes missile systems, rocket motors and the like. General Motors is also active in the aircraft industry through its Allison aircraft engines and defence equipment. Piper aircraft, the light aviation machines much used in business travel and charter hire is American and distributed by CSE Aviation in this country.

Air Holdings has the franchise to sell the US Lockheed L-1011 airbus throughout the world outside the USA.

In the field of aircraft components a number of American owned companies predominate. These include H K Porter; Amphenol-Borg; Cannon Electric, an ITT subsidiary; and British Wire Products which is owned by American Chain & Cable Company of New York.

Avdel, also large manufacturers of aircraft components including industrial fastening devices, was originally an American subsidiary. In the mid-1950's its director sold out his controlling interests to a Swiss concern, Aircraft Investments, and this combine now acts as the holding company of a widely scattered group of factories.

Thorn-Bendix is jointly owned by the British Thorn and the Bendix Corporation of New York and manufactures aircraft electrical components, industrial electronic equipment and pneumatic gauges. This company is expected to expand into such areas as fluidics, fibre optics, oceanography and other diversified aspects. Bendix has designed the central air data computer for installation in the Concorde and is working on an automatic flight control system for supersonic aircraft. The Bendix doppler navigation system is said to fly on more commercial airlines than any other make.

Berg Manufacturing, whose parent is located in Illinois, makes air brakes and equipment at its Cumbernauld factory.

Sperry Gyroscope is the foremost supplier of aircraft and navigation instruments, all aspects of instrumentation, controls and data handling. The company is a division of Sperry Rand.

Kollsman Instruments, another leading firm making and distributing instruments for aeroplanes, is American owned with a New York-based headquarters. Irving Air Chute, which makes air cargo equipment, parachutes and safety equipment, has a Kentucky parent company. General Dynamics Corporation makes aircraft, missiles, space vehicles and a wide range of aero, nuclear, electronic and electrical equipment. This company also has a British subsidiary. Dzus Fastener manufactures metal fasteners with particular application to the aircraft industry. Its head office is in New York and the European trading operations of this concern are based in Farnham, Surrey. Air Trainers, makers of air crew training equipment, is also an American company.

The B F Goodrich Company of Ohio manufactures industrial rubber products and aerospace components and its products are distributed over here by a London subsidiary. The products of the Bonded Structures Division of the Swiss CIBA are also used widely in the aircraft industry.

The contract to build what will be a unique test centre able to subject a complete Concorde airframe to major fatigue tests under controlled conditions of heating and cooling has been awarded to Sulzer Brothers by the Ministry of Technology. Sulzer is the British subsidiary of the large Swiss engineering company.

Hunting Engineering recently signed a marketing and manufacturing agreement with Automatic Timing & Controls of Pennsylvania covering the complete range of ATC weigh-cells and associated electronics. It is expected that UK manufacture will commence in early 1969.

An important company in the defence programme is Rubery-Owen-Rockwell, an Anglo-American concern covering aircraft, missile, rocket engines, electronic and control equipment. Rubery-Owen-Rockwell is owned by North American Rockwell of California and the British Rubery Owen. North American Rockwell is a major manufacturer of defence and electronic control equipment. It is associated with the London firm Bramber Engineering, manufacturer of vehicle suspension springs, has its own London subsidiary, North American Aviation International, and licensing arrangements with a number of British companies including Rolls-Royce.

A firm specialising in glass fibre air freight containers, which are shaped to fit inside different types of aircraft, is Brownline of Hounslow. Brownline is a division of Tridair Industries in California. The container operators, United Cargo, is also American owned. Air Express International which specialises in air cargo is owned by Wings & Wheels Express of New York.

In order to strengthen its position in underwater technology, Ultra Electric has signed an agreement covering technical know-how with the Sparton Corporation of the US. Supramar, the Lucerne-based company which has built the world's largest hydrofoil, is 50 per cent owned by the City Investing Corporation of New York. A smaller Supramar boat operates round the Channel Islands and the company is supplying its models to several overseas navies. Airavia of Shanklin has the British marketing rights for the Russian hydrofoils.

Hoverlloyd, the company formed by Swedish shipping interests to operate cross-Channel services between Pegwell Bay and Calais with SR-N4 hovercraft, is planning to start operations in April 1969.

Vickers has been licensed by General Dynamics of New York to manufacture and sell large ocean data stations and data navigation stations in the UK. This is the first such licence granted by General Dynamics.

Fluidic components are being developed for the aerospace industry by British Aircraft Corporation, Honeywell and Plessey; English Electric is also about to mass produce. C A Norgren is a subsidiary of the British Shipston Engineering, but the company's fluidics division relies a great deal on American technology and know-how. An important American company in this growth industry is Electrosil, a subsidiary of Corning Glass of New York. The following lists out the remaining major overseas interests in the general area of electronic equipment, aircraft components and associated electrical industries, not specifically mentioned in this chapter.

British company	Product range	Parent company
Air-Log	aerospace engineering and electronics	Air-Logistics Corp, California
Aircraft-Marine Products	electronic connectors, wiring devices, solderless electrical terminals	AMP Inc, Pennsylvania
Amphenol	electronic switches, components, connectors	Amphenol Corp, Illinois
Andrew Antenna	microwave aerials and equipment	Andrew Antenna, Chicago
Arrow Electric Switches	electrical equipment, switchgear, wiring devices	Arrow-Hart & Hegeman Electric, Connecticut
BICC-Burndy	electrical connectors	joint subsidiary of Burndy Corporation, Connecticut and British Insulated Callender's Cables
Booker Bowmar	electronic and servo components	joint subsidiary of Bowmar Instruments, Indiana and Bookers Engineering
Bourns (Trimpot)	electronic components	Bourns, California

British company	Product range	Parent company
British Resistor	*electronic heating elements and resistors*	*Carborundum, New York*
Brush Clevite	*electronic components*	*Clevite Corp, Indiana*
Buchanan Electrical	*crimping tools and equipment for electrical and electronic products*	*Buchanan Electrical, New Jersey*
CSF UK	*electronics*	*American Radio Co, New York*
Cambion Electronic Products	*electronic components*	*Cambridge Thermionic Corp, Massachusetts*
Centralab	*electronic components, capacitors, circuits, potentiometers and switches*	*Globe-Union, Milwaukee*
Clare-Elliott	*relays and stepping switches*	*C P Clare, Chicago*
Coltron Industries	*electronic controls for textiles industry*	*Coltron Industries, North Carolina*
Crouzet-England	*switches*	*Crouzet, France*
Daystrom	*electronic test equipment, measuring instruments*	*Heath Co, Michigan*
Diamond 'H' Controls	*electronic switches, thermostats, energy regulators and relays*	*Oak Electro/Netics, Illinois*
Dynamco	*electronic instrumentation*	*Dynamics Corp of America, New York*
Electrical Components	*electrical wholesalers*	*International Telephone & Telegraph*

British company	Product range	Parent company
Erie Resistor	*electronic components, broadcast receiving equipment*	*Erie Technological, Ohio*
W L Gore	*micro-wire for electronics industry*	*W L Gore Associates, Delaware*
Hellermann Deutsch	*electrical connectors*	*Deutsch, Los Angeles*
Knowles Electronics	*magnetic microphones*	*Knowles Electronics, Illinois*
Mallory Batteries	*miniature mercury and alkaline dry batteries, electronic devices*	*P R Mallory, Indiana*
Mallory Metallurgical Products	*electrical contact materials, resistance welding electrodes*	*P R Mallory, Indiana*
Preformed Line Products	*electric transmission line accessories*	*Preformed Line Products, Cleveland*
Sangamo Weston	*electric meters and controls*	*Sangamo Electric, Illinois*
Sealectro	*electronic components*	*Sealectro Corp, New York*
Shure Electronics	*electronics and microphones*	*Shure Bros, Illinois*
Simplex-GE	*electrical switch and control gear*	*joint subsidiary of General Electric of America and Tube Investments*
Square D	*electrical control gear*	*Square D, Illinois*
Teleregister	*electronics and control systems*	*Bunker-Ramo Corp, New York*

14
CHEMICAL INDUSTRY

Like its electronics counterpart, the chemical industry is almost too diversified to be treated as a single industry. The largest companies manufacturing chemicals will be found in the fields of oil and petroleum, food, drugs, textiles and photography. It is now rare for the large undertakings in the chemical industry to concentrate on a single type of product.

Much of the chemical industry comprises British owned companies, but inevitably there are a number of active foreign controlled concerns and, as would be expected, many British companies work through licensing agreements, some of these being reciprocal. Sales abroad of patented inventions and chemical industrial know-how bring almost £50 million in licence fees and royalties into Britain each year.

Only one of the world's ten largest chemical producers is British owned, as the adjacent table reproduced from a survey published in *Chemical age* (27 July 1968) indicates.

Other foreign chemical companies of size include the Swiss CIBA, Geigy and Sandoz; the Dutch Organon, the Italian Mon-

Company	Country of origin	Group sales ($m)
Du Pont	USA	3,102
Union Carbide	USA	2,546
ICI	UK	2,349
Hoechst	Germany	1,671
Monsanto	USA	1,632
Bayer	Germany	1,604
W R Grace	USA	1,576
Dow Chemical	USA	1,383
FMC Corp	USA	1,313
BASF	Germany	1,276

tecatini-Edison – the world's sixteenth largest chemical concern and the German/Belgium Agfa Gaevert. American owned chemical firms are well to the fore: Allied Chemicals (eleventh largest with group sales of $1,276 million), Cyanamid (thirteenth with group sales of $937 million), Olin Mathieson, Pfizer (whose main activities are described in the next chapter) and the chemical interests of the large oil companies particularly Esso Chemicals, the Anglo-Dutch Shell Chemicals, Phillips Petroleum and the like. Oil companies interests are so strong that, after ici, the two largest chemical companies are Shell Chemicals and BP Chemicals. Shell has a larger stake in chemicals than any other oil company.

American investment in the chemical industry, both in Britain and elsewhere, is increasing as is shown in the following table taken from a study on the chemical industry in Western Europe produced by the Economic Research Group of four banks (Midland, Amsterdam-Rotterdam, Deutsche and Société Generale du Banque) in 1967:

| | $ million | | |
	1957	1961	1965
Total capital expenditure of US chemical industry abroad	*1,958*	*1,857*	*3,452*
	234	*277*	*862*
of which:			
EEC countries	*26*	*63*	*147*
other European countries	*48*	*49*	*174*

There is also much outward investment by British companies. ici has a 25 per cent interest with Solvay in Ste Solvic of France which manufactures ethylene dichloride and vinyl acetate. Distugil of France was owned 50 per cent by Distillers and is now a 50 per cent subsidiary of BP, the remainder being Plastugil (25 per cent), Rhône-Alpes (15 per cent) and ERAP (10 per cent). The company manufactures polychloroprene, marked in the UK under the trade name Butachior.

A recent development has been the entry of several big oil companies to the petrochemicals field. British Petroleum recently undertook a major expansion into petrochemicals. The group's new complex includes a 130,000 tons year orthoxylene and 100,000 tons a year paraxylene plants. Both plants will, in fact be operated by BP California, a joint company owned equally by BP and the United States Chevron Chemical Co. Another example of an oil company expanding its interests is the co-operation of Continental Oil of New York with Staveley Chemical and the National Coal Board in a polyvinyl plant, now under construction. Petrofina too is particularly involved in developing its petrochemical interests throughout the world and there is a possibility that the company will extend in this sphere of operations in the UK probably near its recently opened Lindsey refinery. Shell Chemical also has a large petrochemical complex at Carrington. Naphtha is supplied mainly from Shell's 10·25 million ton per annum Stanlow refinery.

In petrochemicals and related areas such as fertilisers, the threat remains, even to the largest companies, that they will be eventually taken over by oil companies. To ward this off chemical firms have already resorted to a number of devices: take-overs, mergers, splitting their petrochemical requirements between many oil companies, even forming joint subsidiaries with oil companies to produce the feedstock they themselves need. Such an example is a recent link between ICI and Phillips Petroleum of Oklahoma.

The linking of British and overseas interests in joint subsidiaries is common in the chemical industry. A good example can be seen in the British Petroleum subsidiary, BP Chemicals, which has acquired a number of chemical interests held by Distillers. One such is British Hydrocarbon Chemicals of which BP formerly held a half share. BHC is itself the parent of two subsidiaries: Grange Chemicals and Forth Chemicals. Forth manufactures styrene monomer and Monsanto holds a one-third stake in the company; Grange makes detergent alkylate and one-third of this company is held by Chevron Chemical Co of San Francisco. Associated Octel is another partly owned subsidiary of BP Chemicals and manufactures lead alkyl anti-knock compounds. Its parentage is made up as follows: BP Chemicals 36·7 per cent; Shell 36·7 per cent; Socal/Texaco 21·3 per cent and Mobil Oil 5·3 per cent. Honeywill-Atlas which manufactures polyurethane and industrial chemicals is owned half by BP and half by Atlas Chemical of Delaware. British Geon, a major producer of vinyl plastics, is now 55 per cent BP (it was also formerly part owned by Distillers) and 45 per cent B F Goodrich of Ohio.

Distillers still maintains its half share in Bakelite Xylonite with Union Carbide holding the remaining 50 per cent but Distrene, which manufactures polystyrene on a large scale, has been sold to Dow, Distillers former partner in the ownership of Distrene. Dow is particularly active in the production of synthetic fibres and this area of operations has been discussed in the section on the textile industry. Midland Silicones, a subsidiary of Albright & Wilson, in which Dow Corning has a 40 per cent interest, is the largest manufacturer of silicones in Europe. The company also makes resins, rubbers, greases, release agents, textile finishes, water-repellents and anti-foaming agents.

Fisons, well known for its fertiliser interests, has a Loughborough subsidiary – Aquitaine-Fisons which it formed jointly with the French Société National Des Petroles d'Aquitaine to develop plastics interests. Fisons also sells some of the Swiss Geigy products under licence, including the weedkiller Prebane. Geigy, one of the fastest growing chemical companies with a turnover in Britain of about £25 million a year, plans to sell agricultural chemicals under its own name instead of the Fisons trademark. A Fisons-Geigy research and development agreement has been terminated and the commercial co-operation the two companies enjoy is currently under discussion. Geigy UK's Industrial Chemicals division has also announced the development of a new plasticiser and is looking into fields such as toiletries for further diversification.

Shellstar is a joint fertiliser and chemicals venture in the UK by Shell and the US Armour. Shellstar is building a £20 million plant in Cheshire which it hopes to have in production at the end of 1968. Shell Chemical Company also has a minority interest in Lankro Chemicals which manufactures non-ionic detergents, emulsifiers, stabilisers, plasticisers and weed killers and is licensed by Argus Chemical Corporation of New York. Armour's other British interests include Whitby Potash which is currently constructing a small pilot plant for potash extraction in Egton Low Moor.

Du Pont's activities as far as the UK are concerned are mostly concentrated in the field of textile fibres which has been discussed in chapter six. Du Pont's foreign investment is nearly $1,000 million, 43 per cent of this being in Europe. The company is listed twelfth in America by *Fortune* and as benefits its size, it has a great variety of product lines, being active in elastomer chemicals, electrochemicals, explosives, packaging film, industrial and biochemical products, organic chemicals, photographic products and so on.

A closer look at the plastics and rubber industries will further show the extent to which the British chemical industry relies on overseas investment and know-how.

The major producers of polythene are ICI, Shell, Monsanto and Bakelite Xylonite. A large quantity of polyethylene is also imported from Japan. ICI is the dominant British producer, but Bakelite Xylonite is currently expanding its production capacity to 80,000 tons per annum.

Monsanto has 3,000 employees or more, two-thirds of its issued ordinary share capital is held by the St Louis parent, the remainder is held by nearly 8,500 shareholders practically all of whom are resident in the UK.

The Monsanto plant in Newport makes petrol additives, antioxidants, detergents, rust and sludge inhibitors and a wide range of plastics and rubber chemicals including ABS/SAN polymers and expandable polystyrene. Monsanto's Fawley plant manufactures low density polyethylene; ethylene-vinyl-acetate copolymers which find wide applications in film extrusion coating; wire and cable covering; pipes and tubes, bottles and containers. The Ruabon plant which has been in operation for more than 100 years manufactures basic organic chemicals covering a wide area of application. Monsanto exports 40 per cent of its UK production and during the year ended 1967, spent about £1·7 million on new plant and facilities in this country. The 50 per cent stake which Monsanto Chemicals had in R H Cole was dropped to 22½ per cent when Cole's became a public company. Cole specialises in processing, compounding and manufacturing thermoplastic moulding powders and colouring systems; the group also supplies chemical and electronic products under a number of agreements with major chemical and allied concerns.

Polypropylene is a plastic material increasingly used to manufacture a wide range of household goods and motor components. ICI's Propathene commands 60 per cent of this market. ICI and Shell hold the exclusive polypropylene licences in the UK from the Italian Montecatini Edison and the German Karl Ziegler.

Reciprocal trading agreements, covering the complete exchange of technical knowledge on plastics containers, were recently signed by Thermo Plastics, the Dunstable-based converter, with three European companies Svein Stronberg of Norway and Friedrich Stuckenbroker and Paul Craemer, both of Western Germany.

A licence agreement also operates between BP Trading, a British Petroleum subsidiary and Du Pont to use the American company's technology and patents for manufacture of low density polyethylene in the UK and Western Germany.

ABS – acrylonitrile-butadiene-styrene is finding a wide application in engineering and household appliances. The world's largest producers of ABS claim to be the Marbon Chemical Division of Borg-Warner. Marbon manufactures at Grangemouth where it opened in 1964 under the trade name Cycolac.

The Borden Chemical Company, a subsidiary of the New York concern of the same name, makes polyester films and laminates and the firm is building a production unit for synthetic resins and formaldehyde near Durham. Rocel, which is a joint subsidiary of Rowland Products of Connecticut and British Celanese is a leading maker of extruded plastic strip. Caligen Foam, whose parent is Tenneco Chemical's General Foam Division, makes polyurethane foam and is active in many aspects of rubber and plastics fabrication.

Epoxy and urethane electrical insulation materials are manufactured by Hysol Sterling, a subsidiary of Hysol Corporation of New York and Sterling Moulding Materials of London. Kent Plastics specialises in moulding, vacuum metalising and furnishing and decorative plastics. Its parent company is in Indiana.

CIBA, the large Swiss company, makes a range of plastics products at its Duxford plant; world sales of this company are more than 2,300 million Swiss francs and it is active in the manufacture of dyes, pharmaceuticals, epoxy resins, rare metals, agro and photochemicals. CIBA is a major shareholder in Clayton Aniline of Manchester which makes a range of dyestuffs; Geigy and Sandoz two more large Swiss owned complexes both have minority holdings in the company.

Acrylic sheeting and moulding powders are made by Lennig Chemicals, a subsidiary of Rohm & Haas of Philadelphia.

Kay Bros Plastics is a part of the Metzeler Group of Western Germany; its subsidiary Foamair makes artificial sponges.

The Dow Chemical Company is the world's largest producer of vinyl chloride monomer and expects to more than double its capacity by 1970. A new latex plant built by Dow operates in King's Lynn.

Scripto, the Georgian-based makers of pens, owns Plasmic which fabricates a range of plastic products; Polypenco which is active in industrial plastics is owned by the Polymer Corporation of Pennsylvania. Polythane Fibres is also American owned and manufactures extruded thread in association with Monsanto. Muehlstein-Northwestern is an American subsidiary; the company processes rubber and plastics.

Another important Anglo-American concern is Spaulding-Russell which makes vulcanised fibre and laminated plastics, it is jointly owned by the British Tullis Russell and Spaulding Fibre of New York. British Vulcanized Fibre of Cheshire is a fully-owned subsidiary of Spaulding Fibre.

International Synthetic Rubber was formed and is financed by eight of the leading tyre companies: Dunlop (British); Firestone (us); Goodyear (us); Michelin (French); Pirelli (Italian); Avon Rubber (British); Uniroyal (us) and BTR Industries (British). ISR which already has a styrene butadiene rubber plant of 130,000 tons per annum capacity is building a styrene monomer plant near Southampton. Styrene monomer, for which the new works will have an initial capacity of 60,000 tons a year, is an important raw material in the production of rubber and plastics. ISR also operates a solution polymerisation plant at Grangemouth producing 50,000 tons annually.

Synthetic resins are manufactured by Schenectady-Midland which is jointly owned by Schenectady Chemicals of New York and Midland Tar Distillers. Synthetic rubber and chemicals are also made by Thiokol Chemicals whose head office is in Bristol, Pennsylvania.

Turning to food chemicals, the largest European producers are probably Bush Boake Allen, a subsidiary of the British Albright & Wilson. One of the major producers of food flavours is International Flavours & Fragrances of New York with a subsidiary in Enfield. The position of IFF is somewhat obscured by the fact that food flavours have technical and commercial relationships with fragrances for the perfumery and cosmetics industries. Flavours have been used in foodstuffs for many years, but the flavour enhancer is of comparatively recent introduction. Flavours and fragrances are also made by Florasynth of Greenford, an American owned company. The best known enhancer is monosodium glutinate, the largest European producer of which is the French company Orsans, in whose Italian plants Nestlé has a large shareholding.

As would be expected, a large proportion of the emulsifiers market is in the hands of companies such as Unilever which recently purchased Reichhold Chemicals. Colgate-Palmolive is a major manufacturer of fatty acid chlorides and N-acyl sarcosinates; Procter & Gamble is active in the production of glycerine and fats.

Citric acid, used as a food acidulant, is made by the American Pfizer and the British John E Sturge. Outside the USA, Pfizer's largest research and production centre is at the group's UK headquarters at Sandwich. Pfizer's British organisation, which was established in 1951, employs 3,500 and spends more than £1·25 million annually on research, is highly diversified. The group operates six divisions and has seven manufacturing plants. Their chemical interests are mainly concerned with producing fine chemicals for the food industry and, together with their minerals, pigments and metals divisions accounts for 24 per cent of group sales.

Modern large-scale processing of food can result in loss of natural colour; in addition the introduction of new processed foods has resulted in a demand for a greater variety of colours to make them distinctive. The largest manufacturers of synthetic dyestuffs are ICI and the German-controlled BASF. An important Swiss owned company which makes synthetic aromatic chemicals in the UK is Givaudan, now part of the Hoffman La Roche group of Basle.

Union Carbide has already been mentioned in connection with its share in Bakelite Xylonite. The company, which is listed as number 21 in the *Fortune* ranking of leading American concerns has three main divisions in the UK – chemical, alloys and engineering products. Chemical products manufactured by Union Carbide include ethylene oxide and derivatives, glycol ether solvent, ethanolamines, polyethylene glycols and the like. Chemicals account for 17 per cent of the group's sales, plastics for 17 per cent, industrial gases commands 19 per cent, metals 14 per cent and carbons 15 per cent. As we go to press it is announced that Union Carbide is to build a plant at Hythe to produce silicone compounds.

Diversey, the Chicago-based company, opened in the UK some ten years ago to produce chemicals, particularly detergents, for industry and agriculture. In a move to expand its British investments Diversey recently acquired the Delsanex group of companies and two industrial soap manufacturers – Polusulphin and James Linday – both formerly owned by Cussons. Diversey manufactures bactericides, metal treatment compounds and associated equipment. The company also has a licensing agreement with Deady Chemical of Kansas City for the production of chemicals and equipment for the control of scale, sludge and algae in boilers and water systems.

Cabot Carbon a subsidiary of the Cabot Corporation of Boston, is the major producer in the UK of carbon black, used mainly in tyre manufacture. The British owned Philblack makes oil-furnace carbon black and also sells under licence from Phillips Petroleum, the Oklahoma-based concern.

Penetone-Paripan which makes chemical degreasers, strippers and similar compounds, is owned jointly by Carson-Paripan, Penetone International of America and C Jungdahls of Sweden. Gerhardt-Penick is a subsidiary of S B Penick of New York and manufactures a range of fine chemicals for the drug industry, the company is also active in the production of insecticides and veterinary products.

Two companies active in the manufacture of colloid chemicals are Acheson Industries and International Colloids. Both are American owned; the latter has recently formed a European subsidiary based in the UK and its manufacturing facilities are to be concentrated at a £200,000 factory under construction in Widnes.

Farbenfabriken Bayer, the large West German chemical manufacturer, has formed a holding company in the UK. Located at Richmond-on-Thames, it has an authorised capital of £700,000. The subsidiaries will continue to trade as separate concerns under their present management, these being Bayer Dyestuffs; Baywood Chemicals; Bayer Fibres (Fibretex); FBA Pharmaceuticals; Haarmann & Reimer and J M Steel which now becomes Bayer Chemicals.

Three important European interests in the chemical industry are Hoechst, Sandoz and Starch Products. Hoechst is the British subsidiary of the German Farbwerke Hoechst and has a number of UK interests including-chemicals, dyestuffs and pharmaceuticals. Sandoz is a Swiss concern, with a head office in Basle, and is active in a wide area of dyestuffs, pigments, textile chemicals and pharmaceuticals. Starch Products is controlled by a Dutch holding company. Its UK board of directors contains five British, two Dutch and one American and it manufactures dextrines, adhesives and chemically treated starches for a wide variety of products. Another Dutch owned company is Novadel whose products include chemicals for the paint and allied industries, powder feeders and flour milling machinery components. Novadel's parent company is Noury & Van der Lande which recently acquired Pure Chemicals from Rio Tinto-Zinc.

International Nickel, which has a Canadian-American ownership, is the world's major single producer of nickel and cobalt and their chemicals. The company is also active in the manufacture of selenium compounds and tellurium. Harshaw Chemicals of Daventry is a large manufacturer of electroplating processes, addition agents for electroplating, industrial cleaners and metal finishing plant. Harshaw's parent company is in Cleveland. Another leading American company is the Delaware-based Hercules Powder. The British subsidiary makes a range of synthetic resins, plasticisers, emulsifiers and industrial defoamers.

W R Grace of New York comes fifty-ninth in the *Fortune* list of leading American companies. It has four British subsidiaries and its interests range from soldering fluxes and packaging materials to chemicals and transportation interests.

Cyanamid of Great Britain, owned by the American Cyanamid Co of New Jersey manufactures pharmaceuticals, toiletries, agricultural feed additives, veterinary products and chemicals. A plant for the manufacture of the hydrodesulphurisation catalysts used in petroleum refining is being constructed at Gosport for Cyanamid which has, up to now, only distributed HDS catalysts in the UK.

Rexall Drug & Chemical Co of Los Angeles is incorporated in the UK as Vantorex and operates through five subsidiaries. Two – Rexpak and Noetechnic Engineering are concerned with plastic packaging items and aerosol valves and components respectively; the activities of the Tupperware subsidiary has been described in the household goods section. The chemicals and pharmaceuticals side of Rexall's activities is handled by Riker Laboratories at Loughborough.

The remaining important overseas investments in the chemical industry are as follows:

British company	Products manufactured	Parent company
ADM Chemicals	industrial and general chemicals	Ashland Oil & Refining, New York

British company	Products manufactured	Parent company
Abbey Chemicals	*gelling agents, stabilisers, and products for the paint and plastics industries*	*National Lead, New York*
Ansul International	*industrial chemicals, dry chemical fire protection equipment*	*Ansul International, Wisconsin*
Avnet Shaw Processes	*chemicals and ceramic moulding equipment*	*Avnet, New York*
Baxter Laboratories	*chemicals and pharmaceuticals*	*Baxter Laboratories, Illinois*
Brush Beryllium	*beryllium and alloys*	*Brush Beryllium, Cleveland*
Chemitrade	*bulk liquid chemicals*	*Steuber, New York*
Clydesdale Chemical (to be changed to Norit-Clydesdale)	*chemicals and pharmaceuticals*	*Norit, Amsterdam (entire share capital acquired in June 1968)*
Crystalab	*water demineralising products (sales only)*	*Crystal Research Laboratories, Hartford Conn*
Drew Chemical (UK)	*marine chemicals, detergents, cleaning compounds*	*Drew Chemical Corp, New York*
Elgin Diamond Products	*diamond abrasive compounds*	*joint subsidiary of Diamond Stylus Co and Elgin National Watch Co of Illinois*
Gamlen Chemical Co (UK)	*industrial chemicals*	*Gamlen Chemical Co, San Francisco*

British company	Products manufactured	Parent company
Harshaw Chemicals	industrial chemicals	Harshaw Chemical Co, Cleveland
International Minerals & Chemicals	industrial chemicals, minerals, fertilisers (sales only)	International Minerals & Chemicals Corp, Illinois
Kawecki-Billiton (UK)	chemicals, metals, alloys	joint subsidiary of Kawecki Chemical Co, New York and NV Billiton, Netherlands
M & T Metallic	electroplating materials	M & T Chemicals, New York
MacAndrews & Forbes	paper board and licorice paste	MacAndrews & Forbes, New Jersey
Thomas Morson	alkaloids, photographic and industrial chemicals	Merck & Co, New Jersey
Morton-Williams	three divisions: Adcotes: adhesives, lacquers and the like for the flexible packaging industry; Polysets: epoxy resin moulding powders; Polymer emulsions and opacifiers	joint subsidiary of Morton Chemical Co, Chicago and Williams (Hounslow) Ltd
Nalco	industrial chemicals	Nalco Chemical Co, Chicago
Pittsburgh Activated Carbon	activated carbons	Calgon Corp, Pittsburgh
R P Scherer	chemicals, pharmaceuticals, filled gelatin capsules	R P Scherer Corp, Detroit

British company	Products manufactured	Parent company
Turco Chemical Products	*industrial cleaning products*	*Purex Corp, California*
Witco Chemical Co which has also taken over Cyclo Chemicals	*latex compounds, metallic stearates, polyester resins, PVA emulsions, solvent adhesives and dispersions*	*Witco Chemical Co, New York*

15
PHARMACEUTICALS

The value of the pharmaceutical industry is more than £300 million. Sales to the National Health Service account for some £97 million, the export market is worth about £70 million, £42 million is accounted for in proprietary medicines and £44 million comprises veterinary medicines, animal feed additives and miscellaneous items. Some £26 million is sold within the industry itself for further processing.

The industry is international. Of the 70 major producers of prescription medicines in the UK 40 per cent or more are British owned, one-third are American, Swiss and French companies account for some 7 per cent each, the remainder are German, Swedish, Dutch and Danish. Overseas owned companies account for some three-quarters of the sales to the NHS. The Sainsbury Committee report quotes the following breakdown for 1965:

	Prescription medicines	Speciality drugs
British owned companies	*40 per cent*	*27 per cent*
US owned companies	*39·9 per cent*	*49 per cent*
Swiss owned companies	*9·3 per cent*	*14 per cent*
other European owned companies	*10·8 per cent*	*10 per cent*

Pharmaceutical exports and patented specialities comprise the major part of direct exports from Britain. Through royalty payments they also account for a large part of the industry's contribution to the balance of payments.

The industry is by no means homogeneous. It is made up of many companies, large and small with diverse characteristics and activities. Well over half the medicines used in Britain are produced by international concerns with control domiciled in other countries; these companies are responsible for nine-tenths of world-wide research from which Britain benefits. Few drug houses confine themselves to prescription products and most have major interests in other fields, from industrial chemicals and plastics to cosmetics, food and drink as other chapters of this book indicate.

Ranked by size, the following are the world's largest pharmaceutical companies, according to *Chemical age* (27 July 1968):

Company	Country of origin	Sales ($million)
Hoffman La Roche	*Switzerland*	*809*
Bristol-Myers	*USA*	*730*
Warner Lambert	*USA*	*657*
Pfizer	*USA*	*638*
CIBA	*Switzerland*	*548*
Geigy	*Switzerland*	*548*
Rexall Drug	*USA*	*532*
Merck	*USA*	*528*
Sandoz	*Switzerland*	*460*
Rhône-Poulenc	*France*	*455*

This next list shows the best known pharmaceutical companies manufacturing in Britain by country of origin:

British companies	American companies	Other foreign owned companies
Ashe Laboratories	*Abbott Laboratories*	*Astra-Hewlett (Swedish)*
Beecham	*Armour*	*Boehringer Ingelheim (German)*
Boots	*Bayer Products*	*CIBA (Swiss)*
	Bristol-Myers	*Geigy (Swiss)*
Burroughs Wellcome	*Cyanamid*	*Hoechst (German)*
Crookes	*International Chemical Co*	*May & Baker (French)*
Fisons	*Johnson & Johnson*	*Organon (Dutch)*
Glaxo (incl Evans Medical; Allen & Hanbury's; British Drug Houses)	*Eli Lilly (incl Dista Products)*	*Roche Products (Swiss)*

British companies	American companies	Other foreign owned companies
ICI	*Merck Sharp & Dohme*	*Roussel (French)*
International Laboratories	*Miles Laboratories*	*Sandoz (Swiss)*
Nicholas Laboratories	*Parke, Davis*	
Reckitt	*Pfizer*	
Vitamins	*Phillips, Scott & Turner*	
Westminster	*Riker Laboratories* *G D Searle* *Smith Kline & French* *E R Squibb* *Upjohn* *Vick* *William Warner* *John Wyeth*	

Since the industry is so diversified, a brief alphabetical description of the major foreign owned companies follows.

Abbott Laboratories, whose parent company is in Illinois, ranks number 287 in the *Fortune* list. The British subsidiary was established in 1937, its UK assets are some £2 million and it employs 300. The company manufactures barbiturates and cyclamates; ethical drugs account for 24 per cent of total sales, hospital products for 20 per cent of sales.

American Home Products Corp, mostly known for its household products in the UK is a leading American drug house. Ethical drugs account for 35 per cent of the group's sales, other pharmaceuticals for a further 17 per cent. Its main British subsidiaries are International Chemical; F R Howard and John Wyeth whose activities are described later in this chapter.

Armour Hess is one of the British subsidiaries of the Chicago-based parent. It has a nominal capital of £650,000 and employs some 200. One of its most familiar products is ACTH, widely used in the treatment of rheumatoid arthritis.

BCA Pharmaceuticals is owned jointly by Berk Chemicals and Cope Allman and is licensed by Rachelle Laboratories of California (a subsidiary of International Rectifier) for manufacture of a low-price 'broad spectrum' antibiotic.

Bristol-Myers, number 167 in the *Fortune* list, is one of America's largest drug houses. The company has a nominal capital of £50,000 and employs 200 in the UK. Well known for its cosmetics and toiletries (which are described in the appropriate section) its most familiar proprietary products are Bufferin, Angiers and Supavite. Ethical drugs make up 20 per cent of sales, proprietary drugs 14 per cent.

The pharmaceutical division of CIBA, the giant Swiss company is especially well known for its work in the treatment of mental disorders and its research into vitamins, hormones and steroids. Its analgesic Cibalgin is a familiar trade name as is Entero-Vioform. The company is also an active manufacturer of animal health products.

Carteret Products, a division of Carter-Wallace is best known for Carter's Little Liver Pills and an indigestion remedy called Solvol.

Crookes, the British pharmaceutical company jointly owned by Arthur Guinness and Philips, has a recently announced link with the American firm William H Rorer. Rorer has contracted with Crookes to manufacture and distribute in the UK its Maalox and Ananese products. Rorer's drugs will be made by Crooke's subsidiary Basingstoke Pharmaceuticals and marketed by Rorer Laboratories of Watford. The contract is estimated to be worth £500,000 a year.

Cyanamid of Great Britain entered the UK pharmaceuticals field in 1945, marketing the ethical products of Lederle Laboratories. Manufacture in Britain started in 1950. Cyanamid is particularly active in antibiotics including the tetracyclines and was responsible for the introduction of Aureomycin. It also makes agricultural and veterinary products and the parent company comes 83rd in the *Fortune* list of large companies.

Although primarily known for its chemicals, Dow is also active in animal health products. In 1967 some 150 million chickens in the UK were treated with Coyden, a disease-control agent.

Ex-Lax, the laxatives manufacturer, is a subsidiary of the New York firm of the same name.

Giegy, the Swiss company, whose details will also be found in the chapter on the chemical industry, introduced the drug Imipramine for the treatment of mental depressions. It has pioneered the use of DDT compounds.

Gerhardt-Penick is a subsidiary of the American S B Penick, which manufactures and distributes a range of pharmaceutical products including the remedy Tums, by licence agreement with Lewis-Howe of Missouri.

International Chemical is a subsidiary of American Home Products of New York, the giant concern which also owns Prestige and John Wyeth *qv*. International Chemical is best known for Anadin analgesic and its Bisodol and Bigmag indigestion products.

Johnson & Johnson is the New Jersey parent of a group of companies which include Johnson & Johnson (Great Britain), Ethicon and Ortho Pharmaceuticals. Johnson & Johnson manufactures baby products, surgical dressings, hospital products including hypodermic syringes and the like. Ethicon is mainly concerned with surgical supplies such as first aid dressings; Ortho Pharmaceuticals makes obstetric and gynaecological products. The company employs 1,500 and has a nominal capital of £2 million. It ranks 159 in the *Fortune* list.

Lennig Chemical is a subsidiary of Rohm & Haas the Philadelphia company and its animal health division, formerly Whitmoyer Reed, became a fully owned subsidiary of Whitmoyer of America in 1963. The latter was taken over by Lennig in 1964.

The large Italian pharmaceutical Lepetit of Milan opened its first British subsidiary in August 1968. The company has a turnover exceeding £45 million, exports half of its output and is considered one of the world's largest drug manufacturers. It has strong links with Dow Chemical Corporation and its best known product is the antibiotic Rifocin-M.

Eli Lilly is listed number 215 in the *Fortune* directory. This company has been in Britain since 1943 and owns Dista Products which it acquired from Distillers. Eli Lilley covers a wide range of medicinal products from vitamins to analgesics. Dista Products was active in the original development of vitamin B12 and is also known for Penspek oral penicillin. The American parent helped to pioneer insulin on a commercial scale in 1921. Eli Lilly is one of the National Research Development Corporation's licensees which is working on the antibiotic Cephalosporin C.

May & Baker of sulphonamide fame is controlled by the French Rhône-Poulenc. It manufactures pharmaceuticals, pesticides, veterinary products and tropical medicines. The company has wide research facilities at its Dagenham laboratories.

Merck Sharp & Dohme is a subsidiary of Merck of New Jersey, one of the world's largest producers of ethical drugs. The company is especially active in antibiotic preparations such as Aldomet (for cardiovascular therapy) and Indocid. Merck, along with Searle and Organon, is pioneering new steroids; it is also concerned with veterinary drugs and vitamin preparations. Early in 1968 Merck merged with the Calgon Corporation which represents 14 per cent of its sales.

Miles Laboratories is best known as the manufacturer of Alka-Seltzer. It carries an extensive range of proprietary and ethical products, has an authorised share capital of £70,000 and is a subsidiary of the Indiana company of the same name.

Organon Laboratories was formed in 1939 as a subsidiary of the Dutch company which is itself an offshoot of the Swanenberg Meat Company. The main Organon products are hormones, steroids and cosmetic hormone creams, all of which this company helped to develop.

One of the first overseas drug houses to come to the UK was Parke, Davis which was founded in the USA more than a century ago. The British subsidiary was opened in 1891 and now employs some 1,350. Parke, Davis is particularly important in the field of steroids and antibiotics, especially chloramphenicol, which was discovered by an American chemist working on a grant from the company.

Ethical and proprietary drugs make up 45 per cent of the sales of Pfizer. Although the American parent dates back to 1848, its British subsidiary was not opened until 1951. The company's drug interests are as wide as its chemical and cosmetics activities since it manufactures antibiotics, vaccines, steroids, animal health products as well as ethical and propriet-ary preparations. Its best known products are Terramycin and Vibramy-cin (both antibiotics), Sabin, the sugar-lump polio vaccine and the anti-septic TCP. Pfizer was one of the first drug houses to exploit the develop-ment of penicillin on a commercial scale. The company collaborates with the Medical Research Council and Glaxo on developing the common cold vaccine, and again, with the MRC and a number of British drug houses, on trachoma vaccines with the backing of the National Research Develop-ment Corporation.

Although not yet active in this sector of British industry, it is interesting to observe that Revlon, the American cosmetics firm, has bought a small share of Norwich Pharmaceutical, a US drug house, its first venture into the field of pharmaceuticals.

Riker Laboratories is one of the two trading divisions of Vantorex whose activities are described in the previous chapter. Riker manufactures a wide range of ethical drugs as well as aerosol packs for the pharmaceutical industry. The company is situated in Loughborough and its parent is in Los Angeles.

Roche Products is owned by the Basle-based Hoffman-La Roche and has been active in Britain since 1908. It manufactures analgesics, sulpho-namides, vitamins and psychotropic drugs and is a brand leader with such tranquillisers as Librium and Valium. The company employs some 850.

Roussel-Uclaf is a French owned company whose British subsidiary was formed in 1956. The group turnover is 734,153,000 Frs and pharmaceuti-cal specialities account for 59 per cent. The company's main specialised groups are drugs, therapeutic chemicals and products for agriculture and cattle rearing. The British company is building a £2 million factory and laboratories at Swindon. Roussel is best known for its corticosteroids.

Sandoz, the leading Swiss chemical complex, recently acquired A W Wander which is particularly active in streptomycins. Sandoz itself makes a wide range of ethical preparations and was responsible for the discovery of the drug LSD in its Basle laboratories.

G D Searle is a Chicago-based company which opened in Britain in 1953. It is currently transferring its production facilities to Morpeth where expansion is planned. Searle is best known for the contraceptive pill Ovulen which is thought to have almost a third of the market. The company is also one of the originators of the steroid drugs and is currently pioneering the use of sex hormones in agriculture under the trade name Syncro-Mate. Searle is equally active in tranquillisers, antihistamines and anticholinergics. Drammamine, used to combat travel sickness, is one of this company's proprietary names.

The Smith Kline & French laboratories at Welwyn Garden City were opened in 1959. The company's head office is in Philadelphia and it manufactures a wide range of proprietary products including Contac cold decongestant and Thorazine tranquilliser. SKF makes ethical drugs; its activities in toiletries and food have already been noted.

E R Squibb is another American drug house which opened in Britain in the post-war period when so many us companies were investing here. It is now associated with the Olin Mathieson Chemical Corporation and produces antibiotics, anti-rheumatic agents, antiseptics, tranquillisers, diuretics, vitamins and veterinary products. Squibb International, the New York parent company is particularly concerned with radioactive pharmaceuticals.

Stafford-Miller is a subsidiary of Block Drug of Jersey City. It manufactures pharmaceutical products and dentifrice fixatives and cleansers including Dentu-Creme, Sonsodyne, Wernet and Poli-Grip.

Sterling-Winthrop is owned by Sterling Drug of New York, but its Surbiton-based subsidiary is virtually autonomous. The company covers interests from pharmaceuticals to household products and has two ethical drugs divisions: Bayer Products which supplies the British market and Winthrop Products, a holding company for Sterling's European operations where the Bayer name belongs to the Germans. Group turnover is around £22 million and the company holds one of the first Queen's awards for exports. A subsidiary company is Phillips, Scott & Turner which is famous for Andrews Liver Salts and Milk of Magnesia. Sterling Drug of America is listed 186 by *Fortune*. Ethical drugs account for 32 per cent of the parent company's sales.

The American firm Upjohn was formed in 1886 and its British subsidiary opened in 1952. It manufactures corticosteroids, antibiotics and veterinary products. The company has a nominal capital of £210,000 and employs 200. It is listed 292 by *Fortune*.

Vick International is owned by Richardson-Merrell of New York, whose other British subsidiary, Merrell-National, also makes pharmaceuticals. Vick is well known for nose and throat preparations such as Formula 44, Therex, Vapo Mist, Primes and Clearsil.

William Warner is one of the subsidiaries of the New Jersey Warner-Lambert Pharmaceuticals and its most familiar trade name is Veganin. The parent company acquired American Optical Company, an important maker of medical and scientific instruments, as part of a diversification programme. Warner-Lambert's 1967 sales were composed as follows: ethical drugs 23 per cent; proprietary preparations 23 per cent; toiletries and cosmetics 8 per cent; foreign sales 33 per cent; American Optical 26 per cent. The British subsidiary employs 1,000 and has an issued share capital of £1 million.

John Wyeth has been in Britain since 1937 and manufactures ethical and proprietary products, the best known being Aludrox, Algipan and Endrine. It also manufactures infant foods and nutritionals. Wyeth's capital is £2 million, it employs some 800 and is owned by the American Home Products Corporation.

16
MACHINE TOOLS

Borg-Warner is currently working with the Cincinnati Milling Machines Company on a system of automatic transmission, a new development in the machine tool industry. This method was developed simultaneously in Birmingham and America and is intended to bring together the benefits of numerical control for small batches of highly mechanised transfer lines in mass production of a wide range of jobs.

Cincinnati is the world's biggest machine tool manufacturer with global sales of £115 million in 1967. Although not the largest British manufacturer, it occupies an important position in the UK market and employs 3,000. The leading UK manufacturer is Alfred Herbert, which although British owned and controlled, is not entirely free from American money. At the beginning of 1968 Herbert formed a partnership with Ingersoll Milling Machine Company of Illinois. The £4·5 million Herbert-Ingersoll factory opened in Daventry at the end of February to produce something in the order of £4·5 to £5 million annually by 1970. Half the equipment is expected to be imported and will consist of special purpose machines including numerically controlled types rather than the conventional machine tools. Alfred Herbert has a 51 per cent holding in Herbert-Ingersoll with the remainder in the hands of the American concern. Alfred Herbert has a machine tool subsidiary Pratt, Whitney & Herbert which it jointly owns with Colt Industries of New York. The link is further strengthened as Herbert also acts as licensee for Colt Industries. Alfred Herbert employs some 12,000. Until recently Alfred Herbert and Charles Churchill have been selling Cincinnati products in the UK, this is about to be altered as the American group is setting up its own factory-trained sales force here.

Another large machine tool manufacturer in the UK is Giddings & Lewis of Wisconsin. Giddings & Lewis-Fraser, the British subsidiary, aims to sell around £2 million worth of equipment on the British market during the next two years as its own direct sales company comes into operation. Currently Giddings & Lewis uses Rockwell Machine Tool Company to distribute its horizontal boring and milling machinery, while its range of ending and centring machines, made at Arbroath, is sold through Sidney G Jones. Giddings & Lewis entered the British market in 1959 when it bought a 51 per cent interest in Douglas Fraser, the manufacturer of jute machinery and specialised machine tools.

In terms of annual sales on a world-wide basis, Giddings & Lewis is ranked second to Cincinnati Milling with a turnover of some £40 million a year. Its British turnover is about £4 million with some £1·5 million derived from overseas sales of textile machinery. It exports a large proportion of its output and its series of horizontal borers, currently manufactured under licence by Schiess of Düsseldorf, will be handled in the UK as soon as the new Altrincham sales office has been established.

A new Anglo-American group has been formed within the British machine tool industry following completion of an involved series of deals. Prime mover in the development has been the Leicestershire firm of Marwin which currently claims to be producing about £4 million worth of nc equipment a year. This company has bought the foundry, machine shop and machine tool building interests of Ashwell & Nesbit which in turn has given Marwin a half share in Snyder, the company already established in the UK with the aid of the Snyder Corporation of Detroit which owns the other 50 per cent. Snyder has itself acquired Viltool of Wolverhampton from Manganese Bronze Holdings. The combined company thus formed is called Snyder-Viltool. The link-up will be highly competitive with Herbert-Ingersoll and will be entering fields where organisations such as Buhr Machine Tool, Kearney & Trecker-CVA and Ex-Cell-O Corp are prominent. Buhr, whose Sutherland works is the UK division of the Michigan parent company, is known for specialised machine tools; Kearney & Trecker-CVA (Kearney & Trecker of Milwaukee owns 65½ per cent of ordinary capital) carries a range of machine tools and accessories, fractional hp motors, jigs, moulds and the like. Ex-Cell-O Corp is active in the field of machine tools and associated equipment. The parent company in Detroit also manufactures dairy equipment. The major British contenders in this area are Staveley Industries, John Brown, George Cohen and Tube Investments.

Another move which could cut Britain's machine tool imports has been put into effect by Wickman which has an agreement with Yoder of Cleveland to make the latter's products in the UK.

Ferranti recently announced a tie-up with the German Grundig to make numerical control equipment for machine tools. The two companies plan to integrate their existing nc ranges and aim to provide joint marketing and servicing throughout the world. Ferranti is particularly strong in the technology of finished systems; Grundig's contribution will be marketing know-how and its own technology on electronic components for numerical control equipment. To date 1,600 machines in Britain have been equipped by numerically controlled methods.

The other overseas investments in the British machine tool industry can best be seen in tabular form:

British company	Product area	Parent company
Ada (Halifax)	Ajax machine tools	Philips Electronic & Associated Industries owns 52 per cent
Aro Corp	air tool and pneumatic control equipment	Modernair, Indiana
Barber & Colman	machine tools, auto controls, mechanical fasteners	Barber-Colman, Illinois
Browne & Sharp	machine tools	Browne & Sharp, Rhode Island
Cleveland Twist Drill	drilling and cutting tools	Cleveland Twist Drill, Ohio
Cone Automatic Machine Co	machine tools	Cone Automatic Machine Co division of Pneumo Industries, Vermont
Consolidated Pneumatic Tool	machine tools, pumps and compressors, portable power tools	Chicago Pneumatic Tool
Frank Guylee	engineers tools	Chicago Pneumatic Tool
Heald Machines	machine tools	Cincinnati Milling Machine
Landis Machine-Maiden	machine tools, threading machines etc	Landis Machine, Pennsylvania

British company	Product area	Parent company
Precision Gear	machine tools, precision equipment	National Broach & Machine Co, Detroit
Ridge Tool	pipe tools, pipe and bolt threading machines and accessories	Emerson Electric, Missouri
Sandvik	machine and specialised tools	Sandvik, Sweden
L S Starrett	precision tools and hacksaws	L S Starrett, Massachusetts
Thor Power Tool	pneumatic and electric	Thor Power Tool, Illinois
Warner Swasey Asquith	machine tools	jointly by Warner & Swasey of Cleveland and Asquith Machine Tool Corp of Halifax
Weatherley-Cincinnati	broaching machines, fixtures and tooling	Cincinnati Milling Machine

17

FRANCHISING AND LICENSING

Franchising is an arrangement whereby an organisation (known as the franchisor) has developed a successful retail product or service and extends, offers or sells to individuals (known as franchisees) the right to engage in the franchisor's business provided they follow an established pattern. A high proportion of franchise operations are underwritten by foreign investment and equipment. Anglowest Laundry Distributors offers Westinghouse equipped coin-op laundry or dry-cleaning shops; Martinising Sales is an American-based dry-cleaning centre; Homecare Distributors is a division of Chemical Associates, another leading USA manufacturer of cleaning equipment. Permaclean is one of the leading services in this country offering on-site carpet and upholstery cleaning franchises and this company has the exclusive distribution rights of American equipment made by Von Schrader.

Although a large amount of franchising takes place in the laundry and dry cleaning fields, it is by no means restricted to this sphere of operations. Claire International is a Canadian owned floral service. Budget Rent-A-Car was founded in Los Angeles in 1958, is now the world's largest discount car hire system and has a UK office in Hounslow. Arnold Palmer is a well-known name in golf and his American company's franchised golf ranges or putting courses operate in Britain. Franchising also extends to education. Success Motivation is a managerial training course system started in the USA by Paul Meyer; Dale Carnegie salesmanship courses are franchised to Leadership Promotions. The employment and staffing agency, Manpower, is also American owned and again operates through regional franchisees.

It is not perhaps realised just how much money flows out of a country in royalty and licensing payments. According to Board of Trade estimates, licensing payments to overseas affiliates for royalties and other services was £60 million in 1966, slightly more than 1965 and represented about 55 per cent of the sum of branch profits, dividend and interest remittances.

A cursory study of company reports read while researching for this book revealed the following

Dividends paid to Eastman Kodak by its overseas subsidiaries during 1966 totalled $16·7 million, an increase of 19 per cent over the previous year. Royalties paid by Eastman Kodak's manufacturing companies overseas (British Kodak is one) amounted to $8·9 million, 11 per cent higher than in 1965. To be fair, the balance was retained outside America to finance current operations.

Royalty receipts from foreign licensees paid to the Bendix Corporation during 1967 totalled $6·4 million compared with $6·1 million in 1966. During 1967, 17 new agreements were executed and at the end of the year the corporation had a total of 472 agreements outstanding with 167 licensees in 19 foreign countries. Royalty receipts show a 100 per cent increase from 1961 to 1967.

Remittances of income and dividends to Eli Lilly & Company by overseas subsidiaries and branches during 1967 was just under $3 million, a one third increase over 1966.

Smith Kline & French's 'goodwill, patents and other intangibles' amounted to more than $15 million in 1967.

CIBA's 1967 income from affiliates was some 31 million Swiss francs, this sum included licence payments, dividend receipts and the like.

The situation is not, of course, peculiar to Britain. Early in 1968 a Senior Czech economic official indicated that a major portion of a gold rouble loan from the Soviet Union would be used to purchase manufacturing licences from the United States and other western countries for the improvement of domestic industries.

It should also be borne in mind that Britain's revenue is substantially increased by licence receipts for its own products. The latest annual report (1966-67) of the National Research Development Corporation quotes receipts of £492,674 from overseas payable to the Corporation alone. Most of this sum was derived from the USA and over two-thirds of the payment came from NRDC's licensing of the antibiotic Cephalosporin. As was indicated in chapter 15 one of the two licensees of Cephalosporin is Eli Lilly, an American-owned company!

The British journal *Product licensing index* is the only one that makes any attempt to list regularly and rationalise the granting of licences.

The following list culled partly from that journal is a brief indication in some licensing agreements operating between British and overseas companies. This list merely scratches the surface of this very involved sphere of operations, but it is an attempt to show, by subject breakdown, the type of equipment which is on the British market as the result of a licensing arrangement. Unless otherwise stated, licensors are American companies.

Licensing agreements

Product	Licensee	Licensor
Abrasives, grinding wheels, electro-chemical material	Morganite Electroheat	Norton Co
Accelerometer	Elliott-Automation	Northrop Corp
Accumulators	Venner	Yardney International
Acrylonitric foam production process	ICI	Sekisui Chemical (Japan)
Adhesive mastics and sealants	Atlas Preservative	Benjamin Foster
Adhesive plastics	Cray Valley Products	General Mills
Advertising	British & International Addressing	Mailograph
Advertising displays and merchandising units	Sackville Smeets	Paper Products Development Corp
Aerosols	Armstrong Laboratories	Aerosol Techniques
Aerospace equipment	*William Warne Palmer Aero Products	R E Darling & Co Resistoflex Corp
Aggregate production plant	Pegson	Smiths Engineering Works
Agitators, industrial	Joseph Winterburn	Chemineer Inc
Air brakes	Clayton Dewandre; Westinghouse Brake & Signal	Bendix-Westinghouse; Automotive Air Brake
Air conditioning, heating, refrigeration, turbines and compressors	Carrier Engineering; Consolidated Pneumatic Tool; J Stone; Stone-Platt Industries	Carrier Corp
Air conditioning, refrigeration and heating equipment	Searle Manufacturing	Dunham-Bush
Air diffusion equipment	Air Distribution Equipment	Titus Manufacturing

*indicates cross-licensing agreement

Product	Licensee	Licensor
Air filters and filtration equipment	Ozonair Air Control Installations	Cambridge Filter Westinghouse Electric International
Aircraft and commercial fasteners	Brown Brothers	Huck Manufacturing
Aircraft instruments and components	KGD Instruments Airtech Westland Aircraft H M Hobson	Trans-Sonic Radar Relay United Aircraft Corp Lockheed Georgia; Abex Corp
	Hawker-Siddeley Dynamics	Hamilton Standard Division, United Aircraft Corp
	Plessey	MSL Industries; General Dynamics
	Vactric Control	Technical Development Co
	Louis Newmark Elliott Flight Automation Teddington Aircraft Controls English Electric; Ferranti; Rolls-Royce Automotive Products; Plessey Smiths Industries Laycock Engineering Teleflex Products	Lear Siegler Honeywell; Northrop Conrac Corp North American Rockwell Corp TRW Inc Eaton Yale & Towne Dana Corp Airborne Accessories
Aircraft propellors	Dowty-Rotol	Curtis-Wright Corp
Airfield ground support equipment	*Mercury Airfield Equipment	Cochran Equipment
Alarm safety devices	John Davis	Electro-Alarm Safety Devices
Alloy castings	Wellman Alloys	Duraloy Co; Blaw-Knox
Aluminium	Kerry's (Ultrasonics); Reads Ltd	Aluminium Co of America

*indicates cross-licensing agreement

Product	Licensee	Licensor
Aluminium fabrications	Archibald Low Arc Aluminium	Liskey Aluminium Northrop Architectural Systems
Aluminium kitchenware	*Mirroware Co	Mirro Aluminium
Architectural light fittings	Rotaflex	Lightolier
Asphalt paper and gypsum products	Bowater Packaging	Fibreboard Paper Products Corp
Asphalt shingles, roll roofings	Clayton Dewandre	Certain-Teed Products
Automation and programming equipment	Hawker-Siddeley Dynamics	Machine & Foundry
Automatic control devices, electronic instruments, data processing	Elliott-Automation	Honeywell; Northrop; Bristol Co; Consolidated Electro-dynamics
Automatic door mats	BMB (Sales)	Bendix
Automatic shut-off valves	Rockwell Flow Controls	Rockwell Manufacturing
Automatic storage systems	Geo W King	Triax
Automatic timers	Everett Edgcumbe	Automatic Timing & Control
Automatic viner feeders	Mather & Platt	Frank Hamachek Machine
Automatic welding and jointing equipment	Bedalex	Sippican Corporation
Automobile body undercoat	H W Chapman	Daubert Chemical
Automobile servicing equipment	Crypton Equipment	Marquetta Corp
Baby clothes	Aristoc	Carter
Bags (packaging)	J & W Baldwin	Jiffi Manufacturing
Ball bearing slewing rings	Dobson Hardwick	Rothe Erde (West Germany)

*indicates cross-licensing agreement

Product	Licensee	Licensor
Bearings and shafts	Ransome & Marles Bearing Co	Thomson Industries
Bedding machinery	P Fanghanel	United Mattress Machinery
Bedframes, divans	Slumberland	Harvard Manufacturing
Bending devices	Bowthorpe Electric	Benfield-Detroit
Bi-metallic products	Wellworthy	Al-Fin Corp
Blast cleaning, finishing and dust control equipment	*Spencer & Halstead	Pangborn Corp
Blast-furnace and ancillary equipment	Newton Chambers	John Mohr
Blast furnace and heavy engineering equipment	Ashmore, Benson, Pease; Hygrotherm	Bartlett-Snow-Pacific
Blowers and air vacuum units	Isaac Braithwaite	Belson Corp
Boilers	Marshall Sons	Cleaver-Brooks; Combustion Engineering
Boilers and combustion equipment	Hamworthy Engineering	Preferred Utilities Manufacturing
Boilers, steam engine, coal pulveriser and stokers	Davey, Paxman	Erie City Iron Works
Bolts, nuts, screws, precision parts	L H Newton; Normalized Bolts	Illinois Tool Works
Bookbinding machines	Smyth-Horne	Berry Machine Co
Box making and printing machines	Henry Simon	Rite Size Corrugated Machinery
Brushes	Loewy Robertson	Fuller Brush Co
Building materials	Millar's Machinery	Master Builders
Burners	Urquhart's	Bloom Engineering
Cables	British Insulated Callender's Cables	Furukawa Electric (Japan)

*indicates cross-licensing agreement

Product	Licensee	Licensor
Camblock and campost	Painton	Newal
Cameras	Avo	Coleman Engineering
Cameras, films and polarising lens and filters	Polaroid (UK)	Polaroid Corp
Carbon black	Philblack	Phillips Petroleum
Carbon black and synthetic rubber	United Carbon Black	United Carbon
Carpet sweepers	Bakelite Xylonite	Bissell Inc
Carpets	Birstall Carpet Co	Mohasco Industries
Carpets and rugs	Rivington Carpets	Cabin Crafts
Cartridge fillers, filter media	Stockdale Engineering	Technical Fabricators
Casting machines and foundry equipment	Albert Mann Engineering	Lobeck Casting Processes
Castings	Integral; Lloyds Sheepbridge Alloy Castings; Henry Simon; Stanton & Staveley	Abex Corp US Pipe & Foundry
Cement and chemical grouting processes	General Descaling	Central Industries (Australia)
Centrifugal de-foaming equipment	Joseph Winterburn	Teknika
Centrifugal fans	Gordon Stevenson	New York Blower
Centrifuges	Thomas Broadbent; *Vickerys	Bird Machine
Chemical and industrial processes	Power-Gas Corp	Leonard Process
Chemical and petroleum process equipment	Horseley-Piggott	Struthers Wells
Chemical and process equipment	Constructors John Brown	Hydrocarbon Research

*indicates cross-licensing agreement

Product	Licensee	Licensor
Chemicals	Atlas Preservative; ICI; A H Marks; Merrill Chemicals	Amchem Products
	Albright & Wilson	Calgon Corp; Ethyl Corp; Reheis; Reichhold Chemicals
	British Resin Products; Fisons Pest Control	Tenneco Chemicals
Chromium diffusion processes	Carronchrome	Heuchrome (France)
Clothing	Gossard	Vanity Corset Co
	Reldan	American Machine & Foundry
Clothing industry machinery	G E Jones	American Safety Table
Coating and laminating machinery	T & T Vicars (Simon-Waldron Division)	Midland-Ross (Waldron-Harting & Ross Engineering Divisions)
Coding, dating and marking equipment	Bielomatic; Eagle Packaging & Printing	Dalemark Industries
Coffee machines	W M Still	Alsdorf Corp
Coil coating installations	Carrier Engineering	Gasway Corp
Coin-operated photo machine	Photome	Auto-Photo Co
Coke ovens and by-products plant	Gibbons Brothers	Wilputte Coke Oven Division of Allied Chemical Corp
Compressed air equipment	C A Norgren	C A Norgren
Compressed air purifiers	Electro-Chemical Engineering	Deltech Engineering
Computer equipment and supplies	Elliott-Automation Advance Electronics	Data Disc Data Technology
Computers	GEC/AEI	Scientific Data Systems; General Electric Co of America

*indicates cross-licensing agreement

Product	Licensee	Licensor
Concrete planes, grinders and saws	E P Allam	Equipment Development
Concrete machinery	Winget	Koehring
Connectors	Plessey	Amphenol
Container-making machinery	Henry Simon	Huntingdon Industries
Containers	John Waddington	Illinois Tool Works
Continuous web and strand processing equipment	Mather & Platt	C A Litzler
Control equipment	Austin S Beech Smiths Aviation Division	Numatics Honeywell
Control gear	MTE Control Gear	R B Denison
Control valves, pressure regulators	Hymatic Engineering Dewrance-Triangle	Kieley & Mueller Black, Sivalls & Bryson
Control systems for stored liquid products	Wm Neill	Microdot
Controls and FHP motors	Westool	Controls Co of America
Convector equipment	Efco-Royce Furnaces	Rolec
Conversion coatings	Silvercrown	Conversion Chemical Corp
Conveying machinery	Stratford Auto Flow Systems	Alvey-Ferguson
Conveyor and processing equipment and systems	Stone-Wallwork	Hewitt Robins Division of Litton Industries
Conveyor systems	Murfitt Bulk Transporters Elliott-Automation Bagshawe	Speed King Manufacturing Borg Fabriks (Sweden) H M Sawrie
Corrugated cardboard boxes	Mountbank Engineering	Kole Enterprises
Corvette sweeper	Motor Rail	Balayeuses Mathieu (France)
Costume jewellery	Bloxidge Bros	Originalities of New York

*indicates cross-licensing agreement

Product	Licensee	Licensor
Couplings and aircraft components	Bell's Asbestos & Engineering	Janitrol Division, Midland-Ross Group
Couplings and tube connectors	Intertechnique	E B Wiggins
Cranes and earth moving equipment	R H Neal	Unit Crane & Shovel Corp
	Wellman Machine	Hitachi (Japan)
Cranes and monorails	British Mono Rail	American Mono Rail
Cryogenic equipment	W B Butterfield	Cosmodyne Corp
Current interrupter head	Bowthorpe Holdings	Kearney-National
Cutting and stacking machines	Francis Shaw	Spadone Machine Co
Cutting tools	Goodyer-Blackburn	Illinois Tool Works
Cylinders (air, hydraulic, heavy duty)	IMI Group	Hydro-Line
Data handling equipment	Mimic Diagrams & Electronics	Rochester Instrument Systems
Data processing equipment	Elliott-Automation	Consolidated Electrodynamics; Data Disc Corp
	Benson-Lehner	Redcor Corp
Deburring tools	Victor Goodyer	Burr-Ban Tool Service
Diaphragms	George Angus	Bellofram Corp
Die handling equipment	Funditor	Hansford Manufacturing
Dieing machines	Cravens Machines	HPM Division, Koehring
Dielectric shields	Weller Engineering	Saf-T-Boom Corp
Diesel engines	Rolls-Royce	NSU/Wankel (West Germany)
	W H Dorman	Colt Industries
	Vickers	Maschinenfabrik Augsburg-Nurnberg (West Germany)

*indicates cross-licensing agreement

Product	Licensee	Licensor
Digital transfer function analyser equipment	Solartron	Boonshaft & Fuch Division, Western Instruments
Direct-current tachometer	Rank Pullin Controls	General Precision
Dock ramp (self-levelling)	John Wallace Engineering	Service Steel & Engineering (Canada)
Domestic appliances	Bendix Home Appliances	Philco-Ford
Domestic heating systems	Chas Winn	Perfecta Organisation (Switzerland)
Doors, windows, shopfronts	Arc Aluminium	Northrop Architectural Systems
Dough mixing systems	Henry Simon	Baker Process Co
Drafting system	Balmes	Saco-Lowell
Drapery hardware	Antiference	Kirsch
Draught inducers	G Applegate	The Wing Co
Drilling equipment	Kestner Evaporator	Drilling Engineering
Drying equipment	Joseph Winterburn Simon-Waldron	AER Corp Midland-Ross Corp
Drugs and pharmaceuticals	Smith Kline & French	Norwich Pharmaceutical
Dual duct mixing units	Powell Duffryn	Buensod-Stacey Corp
Dust collectors, air cleaners	Harvey Fabrication Clarke Chapman	Torit Corp Siemens (W Germany)
Dust control equipment	Ozonair	Ducon Co Inc
Dust pan	Creators	Foley Manufacturing Co
Earth drilling equipment	BSP-Caldweld	Caldweld Inc
Earth-moving equipment	Osborn-Hadfields	Esco Corp
Electric brakes and clutches	Westool	Warner Electric Brake & Clutch
Electric hoists and series cranes	Clyde Crane & Booth	Pintsch Bamag (West Germany)

*indicates cross-licensing agreement

Product	Licensee	Licensor
Electric motors and generators	Mawdsley's Head Wrightson	Louis Allis Co Bogie Electric Manufacturing
Electric paint sprayer, power and engraving tools	Burgess Products	Burgess Vibrocrafters
Electrical appliances	Automotive Products	Borg-Warner
Electrical controls	Brookhirst Igranic	Cutler-Hammer
Electrical equipment	Auto Diesels; Frederick Braby Albright & Wilson Delaney-Gallay Ross Courtney	Link-Belt Division, FMC International General Electric Robintech Thomas & Betts
Electrical generation, transmission, control apparatus, equipment and turbines	Chilton Electric Products; Plessey; Sturtevant Engineering	Westinghouse Electric International
Electrical instruments	Electronic Instruments	Keithley Instruments
Electrical insulating materials	Langley London	Precision Paper Tube
Electro-photographic zinc oxide	Imperial Smelting	American Zinc, Lead & Smelting
Electronic components	Varelco	Elco Corp
Electronic control systems	Plessey	Bunker-Ramo Corp
Electronic equipment	Advance Electronics Claude Lyons Plessey *Elliott-Automation	Data Technology Corp; Houston Instruments; Zeltex; Medistor Instrument Co Intercontinental Instruments Sippican Corp; Illinois Tool Works; Sonotone Corp; Fairchild Camera & Instrument

*indicates cross-licensing agreement

Product	Licensee	Licensor
Electronic instruments	Morganite Resistors McKettrick-Agnew	Beckman Instruments Scientific-Atlanta
Electric systems, sub-systems and components	Barr & Stroud; British Aircraft Corp; Hawker-Siddeley Dynamics Rotax	Hughes Aircraft D H Baldwin
Electronics	Bonochord Marconi Radiovisor Parent	Colorsound Airtron Division, Litton Industries Robotron
Electronics, oceanics, automotive, aerospace, automation	cross licensing agreements: Elliott-Automation; Stone-Platt Industries agreements: Lucas Gas Turbine; Anthony Pratt licensees: Adwest Engineering; Automotive Products; BMB (Sales); Clayton Dewandre; Decca Navigator; Eaton Axles; Newman, Hender; Normalair; Plessey; Rotax; Thorn Electrical; Vokes; Zenith Carburettor	Bendix Corp
Electroplating addition agents	M L Alcan	Electrochemical Products
Electroplating chemicals	Cruikshank's Division, Forestal Industries	Allied Research Products Division, Richardson Co; M & T Chemicals
Electroplating processes	M L Alkan	Du Tone

*indicates cross-licensing agreement

Product	Licensee	Licensor
Electrostatic painting equipment	Henry W Peabody (Industrial)	Ransburg Electro-Coating
Engine and gear-case accessories	Vactric Control	Technical Development Co
Engine rebuilding equipment	Gray & Campling	BB&W Machine Products
Engineering equipment	F W Brackett; Lancaster & Tonge GKN Engineering Equipment	Zurn Industries Unimation
Engines (outboard)	F Perkins	Oliver Corp
Excavating and logging equipment	Rhymney Engineering	Hydraulic Machinery Co
Expandible polystyrene foam moulding equipment	Lily Cups; William Thyne	Crown Machine & Tool
Expansion joints and flexible metal connectors	C A Parsons	Zallea Bros
Fabricated aluminium products	Hestair Sherpa	Kaiser Aluminium & Chemical Corp
Fastenings (screw thread)	Armstrong Grundy	Heli-Coil Corp
Fasteners	Linread T J Brooks	Illinois Tool Works; Continental Screw Elastic Stop Nut Corp
Ferrous castings and quarry equipment	Armstrong Whitworth (Metal Industries)	Blaw-Knox
Fibre glass and plastics	English Electric	Universal Moulded Fiber Glass Corp
Filters (mechanical)	Plessey	Kukusai Electric (Japan)
Filters and separators	Automotive Products	Purolator Products
Filtration systems	National Standard Lancaster & Tonge	Per Corp Serfilco
Fine boring tooling	Precision Gear Machines & Tools	Briney Manufacturing

*indicates cross-licensing agreement

Product	Licensee	Licensor
Floor maintenance equipment	*Newton Chambers*	*Keltec*
Flow measurement control systems	*Kent Industrial Instruments*	*Potter Aeronautical Corp*
Fluid heating furnaces	*Heurtey*	*Petro-Chem Development*
Fluorographic materials	*Commercial Process Co; Eadon Engraving; East Midland Engravers; Fleetway Printers; Grafika; Palatine Engravers; Scottish Studios & Engravers; Service Engraving; Star Illustration Works; Star Process Engineering*	*Printing Arts Research Laboratories*
Fluxes for light alloys, ferrous and non-ferrous metals	*Berk*	*Aikou Rim-Blox (Japan)*
Folding cartons	*Tillotsons (Liverpool)*	*Interstate Folding Box Co*
Folding doors	*Home Fittings (GB)*	*New Castle Products International*
Folding walls	*British Werno*	*Federal Folding Wall Corp*
Food and beverage	*W & A Gilbey*	*Heublein*
Food processing equipment	*Metal Units Clarke-Built*	*Koch Supplies Girton Manufacturing*
Food processing machinery	*Gordon-Johnson-Stephens*	*Gordon Johnson*
Food products	*H S Whiteside*	*Bachman-Jack's Division, Helme Products*
Food (sauce)	*Horlicks*	*McIlhenny*

*indicates cross-licensing agreement

Product	Licensee	Licensor
Forged alloy-steel teeth for excavating equipment	Ruston-Bucyrus	H & L Tooth
Forging machinery	Alfred Herbert	Chambersburg Engineering
	Loewy Robertson	National Machinery
	Heenan Group	General Dynamics
Forgings	BSA Electrochemical Machines	Steel Improvement & Forge Co
Fork lift trucks	Dobson Hardwick	Schmiedag (West Germany)
Foundation garments	Gossard	Corde de Parie; Tru Balance Corsets
Foundry cleaning and dust equipment	Powell Duffryn	W W Sly Manufacturing
Foundry processes	GKN Engineering	V/O Licensintorg (USSR)
Fresh water distillation units	George Clark & Sons	American Machine & Foundry
Friction materials	Ferodo : Sheepbridge Engineering	Abex Corp
Fume-handling fans	Capper-Neill	Anti-Corrosive Pipe & Lining (Australia)
Furnace equipment	Stein Atkinson Stordy	Rust Furnace
Furnaces	Gibbons Brothers	Holcroft
	GWB Furnaces	Northrop Corp
	Head Wrightson	Salem Brosius
	Wellman Incandescent Furnace	Whiting Corp; H K Porter
	BISRA ; Metalectric Furnaces	Consarc Corp
Furniture	Greaves & Thomas	La-Z-Boy Chair Co
Furniture castors	Archibald Kenrick	G F Shepherd (Australia)
Garden tools	Mitchel & King	Wallace Manufacturing

*indicates cross-licensing agreement

Product	Licensee	Licensor
Gas appliances	Van Engineering	Caloric Corp
Gas bearing gyros	Elliott-Automation	Autonetics Division, North American Aviation
Gas burners	Wellman Incandescent Furnace	Red Ray Manufacturing
Gas cleaning and dust collection equipment	Head Wrightson	Research-Cottrell
Gas equipment	L P-Gas Equipment Old Park Engineering	Bastian-Blessing Progas (Netherlands)
Gas liquefaction plants	Power Gas	L'Air Liquide (France)
Gas/liquid separators, gas/solid filters	Premaberg	Peerless Manufacturing
Gas turbines	John Brown	General Electric Co of America
Gayco classifiers	Davidson	Universal Road Machinery
Gears	David Brown Gear Industries	Zurn Industries
Gear boxes, mechanical power transmissions and assemblies	Hobourn Aero Components NMC Gears Reliance Gear Rolls-Royce Turner Manufacturing	Snow-Nabstedt Gear Corp Simmering-Graz-Pauker (Austria) Illinois Tool Works General Motors Clark Equipment
Gear drives	Varatio Strateline Gears	Airborne Accessories
Generators, waveform synthesisers	Advance Electronics	Exact Electronics
Glass-cutting equipment	Pilkington	Ashai Glass (Japan)
Glass-lined sealed storage structures	Howard Harvestore Products	A O Smith Corp

*indicates cross-licensing agreement

Product	Licensee	Licensor
Glassmaking machinery	Glassworks Equipment	General Glass Equipment
Gramophone records	Pye	Hanna-Barbara Records Sales
	Transatlantic Records	Audio Fidelity; Everest; Prestige
Grinding equipment	Kemworthy Tools	Harig Manufacturing
Grinding machinery	Coventry Gauge & Tool	Thompson Grinder Co
Grip-stripe waistbands	H G Graham	Quick Service Textiles
Hardware	*Stanley Works	Amerock Corp
Harvesting and food processing machinery	Purdy Machinery	Chisholm-Ryder
Hats	Failsworth Hats Associated British Hat Manufacturers	Hat Corp of America John B Stetson Co
Heat dissipating components	Lectropon	International Electronic Research
Heat exchangers	Brown Fintube (UK) A F Craig Birwelco	Brown Fintube Hudson Engineering Yuba Heat Transfer Corp
Heat processing equipment	Priest Furnaces; Whessoe Efco-Royce Furnaces	Selas Corp Lanly Co
Heat sealing devices	Reed Corrugated Cases	Boise Cascade
Heat spraying nozzles	Westool	Delavan Manufacturing
Heat transfer materials	Premaberg	Thermon Manufacturing
Heating and cooling equipment	British Furnaces	Midland-Ross Corp
Heating and plumbing equipment	Mitchell Craig Pumps	Crane Co
Heating and ventilating equipment	Ozonair Engineering J Stone	Ilg Industries Vapor Corp

*indicates cross-licensing agreement

Product	Licensee	Licensor
Heating appliances	London Kingsway	Space Conditioning
Heating, drying and cleaning equipment	NV Tools	Herbert Products
High expansion foam equipment	Merryweather	E W Bliss
High pressure hoses, hand tools	Hill & Co (Tools)	Imperial-Eastman
High temperature fibrous materials	Chemical & Insulating Co	Hitco
High vacuum distillation equipment	Edwards High Vacuum	Arthur F Smith Co
Highway flashers	Dorman & Smith	R E Dietz
Hinges	NV Tools	Soss Manufacturing
Hospital air conditioning equipment	Air Control Installations	Svenska Flaktfabriken (Sweden)
Hospital equipment	Honeywell Controls	American Steriliser
Hot water generators	British Steam Specialities	Aerco Corp
Hydraulic equipment	Amal	Hydro-Line Manufacturing
	Oliver Machinery	Beatty Machine & Manufacturing
	Tecalemit	Globe Hoist Division of Symington-Wayne
	Telehoist	Heil Co
Hydraulic jet and tank cleaners, injectors, valves, marine winches	C P Equipment	Sellers Injector Corp Division, Purex
Hydraulic power transmission	Keelavite Hydraulics	Ex-Cell-O Corp
Hydraulic presses	Gaston R Marbaix Fielding & Platt	Abex Corp General Dynamics
Hydraulic presses, press brakes, guillotines	Auxiliary Rolling Machinery	Ursvikens Mekaniska Verkstads (Sweden)

*indicates cross-licensing agreement

Product	Licensee	Licensor
Hydro-filter dust collectors	August's	National Dust Collector
Ice cream vending machines	National Automatic Machines	Fred Hebel Corp
Impact forging machinery	Alfred Herbert	Chambersburg Engineering
Incinerators	Silas Hyde	C E & I Brule
Indexing units	Aylesbury Automation	Tangen Drives
Indicator systems	Airtech	Radar Relay
Induction heating and melting equipment	Loewy Robertson	Ajax Magnathermic
Industrial and construction machinery	Locker Industries; Vokes	Rex Chainbelt
Industrial cleaning compounds and equipment	Electro-Chemical Engineering	Solventol Chemical Products
Industrial controls	Elliott-Automation	Fisher Governor
Industrial equipment and components	George Angus; Armstrong Patents; Carr Fastener; Gough; Plessey; Pressac; Pyrene; B Thornton; John Watson & Smith; Watson & Sons (Electro-Medical)	Resources & Facilities Corp
Industrial plant and equipment	Henry Balfour; Head Wrightson; West's (Manchester)	Arthur G McKee
	Head Wrightson; International Combustion	Hardinge Bros
Industrial tools	G D Peters	Houdaille Industries
Infra-red equipment	L A Mitchell	Fostoria Corp
Infra-red heaters	GWB Furnaces	Hi-Shear Corp
Injection moulding and diecasting machines	Cravens Machines	Koehring

*indicates cross-licensing agreement

Product	Licensee	Licensor
Insect destroying equipment	Henry Simon	Gardner International
Inserts and studs	Instrument Screw Co	Rosan
Instruments	Elliott-Automation	The Bristol Co
Instrumentation	Negretti & Zambra	Hagan Controls Corp, Division Westinghouse Electric
	Heenan & Froude	Eaton Yale & Towne
Integrated process equipment for chemical and metallurgical treatment of metals	Brightside Engineering	Comec (France)
Internal combustion engines	Rolls-Royce	Continental Motors
Ion-exchange equipment	William Boby	Ashai Chemical (Japan)
Iron and steel sheets	APV-Paramount	Armco International
Knit wire mesh and pot scourers	Stephenson, Mills	Metal Textile Co
Labelling system	Lamson Paragon	Dymco Industries
Labels	William Sessions	Avery Products
Laboratory equipment	Electronic Instruments	Fisher Scientific
Latex foam	Vitafoam	Chemetron
Laundry machinery	Thomas Broadbent	Hydraxtor; Troy Division of Amatek
Lawn mowers	Qualcast	Eaton Yale & Towne
Lifting jacks and chain hoists	Consolidated Pneumatic Tool	Duff-Norton
Lighting equipment	Troughton & Young	Rambusch Decorating
Lime kilns	Gibbons Brothers	Material Development
Limit switches	MTE Control Gear	R B Denison Manufacturing
Liquid level gauges and valves	Bailey Meters & Controls; Jerguson-Tress	Jerguson Gage & Valve

*indicates cross-licensing agreement

Product	Licensee	Licensor
Locking and special fasteners	Normalized Bolts; Ormond Engineering; Charles Richards	Maclean-Fogg Lock Nut
Locomotives (diesel hydraulic) and loaders	Motor Rail	E C Lenning (S Africa)
Low temperature processing equipment	Applied Research & Engineering	Process Plants Corp
Lubricating equipment	Exactor Sterling	Trabon Lubricating Systems
Lubricating systems	Tecalemit Farvalube	Bijur Lubricating Corp Eaton Yale & Towne Inc
Machine tool accessories	Rotax	Scully-Jones
Machine tools	Brooke Tool Manufacturing Precision Gear Machines & Tools Alfred Herbert Horstmann Gear Catmur Machine Tool High Precision Equipment; Rockwell Machine Tool Kearney & Trecker – CVA Victor Goodyer	Giddings & Lewis Lees-Bradner Colt Industries; Fellows Gear Shaper Milman Engineering Moore Special Tool US Baird Corp Lodge & Shipley; Houdaille Industries J E Wood
Machine tools and bending machines	Chamberlain Group	Pedrick Tool & Machine
Machine tools, earth moving equipment, textile machinery	Elliott-Automation	Warner & Swasey
Machine tools, materials handling equipment	Precision Gear Machines & Tools	F Jos Lamb (FAB-TEC)
Machine tools, pneumatic equipment, speed drives for aircraft	Coventry Gauge & Tool; English Electric; Shipston Engineering	Sunderstrand Corp

*indicates cross-licensing agreement

Product	Licensee	Licensor
Machinery and steel products	*Armstrong Whitworth; Constructors John Brown; Rose, Downs & Thompson; Wellman Alloys; Head Wrightston*	*Blaw-Knox*
Magnetic detectors	*Vactric Control Equipment*	*Technical Development Co*
Magnetic materials	*Plessey*	*Arnold Engineering*
Magnets, magnetic products, ceramic insulators	*Plessey*	*Indiana General Corp*
Marine and stationery diesel engines	*Drypool Engineering & Dry Dock*	*Appingedammer Bronsmotorenfabriek (Netherlands)*
Marine boilers	*Superheater Co*	*Combustion Engineering*
Marine engines	*Richardsons Westgarth*	*Sulzer (Switzerland)*
Marking machines	*Mark-O-Print*	*Adolph Gottscho*
Materials handling	*Steelfab*	*Meyer Manufacturing*
Materials handling and construction equipment	*John Allen & Sons*	*Grove Manufacturing*
Materials handling and passenger conveying equipment	*Richard Sutcliffe*	*Stephens-Adamson Manufacturing*
Materials handling equipment	*Powell Duffryn Pressoturn*	*Dempster Bros Tote Systems, division of Hoover Ball & Bearing*
Mechanical equipment	*Moodyplant* *GKN Engineering*	*American Road Equipment Unimation*
Mechanical fasteners	*Firth Cleveland Barber & Colman Salterfix Carr Fastener*	*Tinnerman Products Illinois Tool Works Waldes Kohinoor Illinois Tool Works*

*indicates cross-licensing agreement

Product	Licensee	Licensor
Mechanical handling equipment	Lansing Bagnall Locker Industries	Towmotor Corp North American Rockwell; Rex Chainbelt; Orville Simpson
Mechanism to convert lift trucks to mobile crane and hoist	William E Cary	Jos Dyson
Metal cleaning chemicals and equipment	Henry W Peabody	Kolene Corp
Metal cutting and finishing tools	Birmingham Tool & Gauge; Denbro	Madison Industries
Metal cutting machines	Francis W Birkett	Stone Machinery
Metal cutting tools, automotive test equipment	Brooke Tool	Goddard & Goddard
Metal finishing compounds	Pyrene Co	Rust Proofing & Metal Finishing
Metal finishing equipment	Electro-Chemical Engineering	McDermid
Metal finishing processes	Albright & Wilson	Hanson-Van Winke-Munning
Metal processing equipment	Albert Mann Engineering Marshall Richards Machine	Loma Machine Manufacturing Fenn Manufacturing
Metal products	Casco Mixing Machines	Kol
Metal scrap processing machinery	Sheppard & Sons	Harris Press & Shear
Metal treatment equipment	Rolls-Royce Brightside Engineering	Whitfield Laboratories Stamco Inc
Metal working machinery	High Precision Equipment Marshall Richards Machine	Taft-Peirce Manufacturing Nouvelle Spidem (France)

*indicates cross-licensing agreement

Product	Licensee	Licensor
Metallux technique	*Plessey*	*Electronica Metallux (Italy)*
Metering dispenser	*Albert Stubbe*	*Dosamatic Dispenser*
Metering pumps	*Mitchell-Craig*	*Milton Roy*
Mica paper	*Langley London*	*Mica Paper Division, Acim Paper Corp*
Microjoining equipment	*K & N Electronics*	*Wells Electronics*
Microwave tubes	*M-O Valve Co*	*Microwave Electronics*
Milk and other liquid packaging and dispensing systems	*Reed Corrugated Cases*	*Polygal*
Milling machines (portable)	*Scottish Machine Tool Corp*	*Atlas Portable Equipment*
Mining machinery	*Armstrong-Whitworth Secoma Drilling Equipment* *John Bedford*	*Overstrom; Straub Secoma (France)* *Gardner-Denver*
Missile and space equipment	*Flight Refuelling*	*Hayes International Corp*
Mixers	*L A Mitchell*	*Skinner Engine*
Modular tooling	*Badalex*	*Dixon Automatic Tool*
Motor accessories	*Laycock Engineering*	*Sprague Devices*
Motor speed controls	*GEC (Electronics)*	*Borg-Warner Controls*
Multimeters (electronic)	*Smiths Industries*	*Goerz Electro (Austria)*
Navigation aids and equipment	*Decca Navigator* *Ferranti* *Vactric Control Equipment*	*ITT* *General Precision* *Norden Division, United Aircraft*
Newspaper presses	*Gordon & Gotch*	*Buhler (Switzerland)*
Non-ferrous metal melting furnaces	**Morganite Crucible*	*J A Kozma*

*indicates cross-licensing agreement

Product	Licensee	Licensor
Non-ferrous windows, doors, curtain walls and architectural work	Frederick Sage	General Bronze Corp
Numerical control equipment	Plessey	Bendix Corp
Ocean navigation stations	Vickers	General Dynamics
Oceanographic instruments	Plessey	Bissett-Berman
Office supplies	Carbon Paper Supply Twinlock	Kee Lox Manufacturing Krauth & Benninghofen
Oil and chemical plant and pipelines	Constructors John Brown	Blaw-Knox
Oil and gas wellhead equipment	Wallwork Gears	Oil Center Tool Division, FMC Corp
Oil and water separating machines	A Johnson	Surface Separator Systems
Oil burners	London Kingsway	Controls Company
Oil filters	Powell Duffryn	Maremont Corp
Oil mist collector	Air Control Installations	American Air Filter
Oil purifying equipment	Birfield * Twilflex Couplings	Hilliard Corp
Oil well specialities	Oil Well Engineering	Baker Oil Tools
Oilfield equipment	Wallwork Gears Ruston & Hornsby Capper-Neill; Wm Neill	Cardwell Manufacturing Gray Tool Metrol Corp
Oils and fats production and processing equipment	Rose, Downs & Thompson	Blaw-Knox; Votator Division, Chemetron
Omniguard system	Richardson Westgarth	Thomas A Edison Industries
One-time carbon paper and electronic products	Marconi Instruments	Pacific Industries
Ore milling machinery and equipment	Head Wrightson; Pegson	Mine & Smelter Supply

*indicates cross-licensing agreement

Product	Licensee	Licensor
Orifice fittings	Premaberg	Daniel Industries
Ovens (industrial)	General Engineering	Michigan Oven
Ovens (low-temperature)	Efco Furnaces	Lanly Co
Ozone generators	B Thornton	Invex; Rust Proofing & Metal Finishing
Packaging	Bowater Packaging; Transparent Paper Mardon, Son & Hall Bowater Packaging	Continental Can Mead Corp Scholle Container Corp
Packaging (incl containers)	Betts; Bakelite Xylonite; E S & A Robinson	American Can
Packaging machinery	*DICO Packaging Engineers Bowater Packaging Wright Machinery	MRM Peerless Machine & Tool Salvo Machinery
Paint and varnish	Berger, Jenson & Nicholson Carson-Paripan	Cook Paint & Varnish Co Valspar Corp
Paint strippers	Jenolite	Beck Equipment & Chemical
Paints and chemicals	Berger Jenson & Nicholson	Pittsburgh Plate Glass
Paper	Clyde Paper Inveresk Paper James Barnes	Champion Papers Oxford Paper Cromwell Paper
Paper containers	Liquid Packaging; Waddington; Metal Box	Ex-Cell-O-Corp
Paper converting and plastics extrusion machinery	Bone Brothers	Frank W Egan
Paper converting equipment	Fords (Finsbury)	John Dusenbery Co

*indicates cross-licensing agreement

Product	Licensee	Licensor
Paper finishing machinery	Sir James Farmer Norton	Appleton Machine
Paper industry equipment	*Vickerys	Bauer Bros
Paper machinery	Watford Engineering Works	Rice Barton
	Walmsley (Bury) Group	Clupak
Passenger conveyors	Sutcliffes	Stephens-Adamson
Pea harvesting equipment	Mather & Platt	Frank Hamachek Machine
Pelleting machines	Henry Simon	California Pellet Mill
Petrol pumps and bulk meters	Wayne Tank & Pump	A O Smith Corp
Petroleum products, chemicals	Fisons Pest Control	Gulf Oil
Pharmaceuticals	Gerhardt-Penick	Lewis-Howe; Tri-Kem Corp
Photoelectric switches, readers	Elliott-Automation	Invac Corp
Pipe and cable detectors, electronic equipment	Bruce Peebles Industries	Fisher Research Laboratory
Pipe benders	Bowthorpe Holdings	Benfield-Detroit
Pipe joints	Yorkshire Imperial Plastics	Kunststoffwerk Gebr Anger (West Germany)
Pipe line filters	Lancaster & Tonge	Filterite Corp
Pipe line repair fittings	Premaburg	Pipeline Development
Pipe-wrap materials	Nayler (Petroseals)	Plymouth Rubber
Pipes	Pipe Conduits	Midwesco Enterprises
Piping maintenance machines and tools	Premaburg	T D Williamson
Plant for liquefaction and re-evaporation of natural gas	Power-Gas	L'Air Liquide (France)

*indicates cross-licensing agreement

Product	Licensee	Licensor
Plastic foam laminations	Lintafoam	Hicks & Otis Prints
Plastic hardware	Vactric Control Equipment	Kearfott
Plastic windows	Crittall-Hope	Dynamit Nobel (West Germany)
Plastics and chemicals	Lankro Chemicals	Argus Chemical Corp
Plastics manufacturing process	English Electric	Universal Moulded Fiber Glass Corp
Plating and polishing equipment and supplies	Albright & Wilson; M L Alkan; Forestal Industries	M & T Chemicals
Pneumatic and hydraulic equipment	Drallin Industries	Juvenal et Cordier (France)
Pneumatic control systems	Austin S Beech	Numatics
Pneumatic conveying equipment	Callow Engineering	Ducon Co
Pneumatic partitions	British Werno	Air Wall Division, Hupp Corp
Pneumatic windshield wipers and accessories	Laycock Engineering	Sprague Devices
Polytetrafluoroethylene	Fluorplast	Pampus (West Germany)
Portable construction equipment	E P Allam	Racine Hydraulic & Machinery
Potentiometric recorders	Smiths Industries	Goerz Electro (Austria)
Potentiometers for use in precision servo systems	Elliott-Automation	Fairchild Controls
Power supply units, solid state inverters and converters	Photain Controls	Sanken Electric (Japan)
Power supply units (high voltage)	Ferranti	Wabash Magnetics

*indicates cross-licensing agreement

Product	Licensee	Licensor
Pre-printed tapes and symbols	Chart-Pak	Chart-Pak
Precious metals deposition processes and chemicals	Silvercrown	Technic Inc
Precision hydraulic plate shears	Press & Shear Machinery	Boyeler (Switzerland)
Precision instrument components	Reliance Gear	PIC Design Corp
Precision measuring devices	Horstmann Gear	Taper Micrometer
Precision meters	Claude Lyons	Millivac Instruments
Precision slitting machine	Ford (Finsbury)	John Dusenbury
Precision strain gauges	Welwyn Electric	Micro-Measurements
Preparation plant and equipment	Sturtevant Engineering	Heyl & Patterson
Presses and die sets	English Electric	Danly Machine Corp
Presses, disintegrating machinery	Automatic Baling	Centriblast Corp
Pressing machines	Isaac Braithwaite	Rheem International
Pressure strainer (automatic)	F W Brackett	Zurn Industries
Printed circuits (flexible)	Painton Joseph Lucas	G T Schjeldahl Sanders Associates
Printers' accessory equipment	Victory-Kidder	Mosstype Corp
Printing accessories	NV Tools	Baldwin-Gegenheimer
Printing machinery	Funditor	Challenge Machinery
Printing press dryers	Carrier Engineering	B Offen
Printing presses	Baker Perkins	Wood Newspaper Machinery
	Victory-Kidder	Kidder Press

*indicates cross-licensing agreement

Product	Licensee	Licensor
Process materials	Pyrene	J N Tuttle
Processing equipment and plant	Dorr-Oliver	Komline-Sanderson Engineering
	Henry Simon	Midland-Ross Corp
	Head Wrightson; International Construction	Treadwell Corp
	Head Wrightson	Blaw-Knox
	*International Construction	Galigher Co
	Mather & Platt	Emhart Corp
	L A Mitchell	C G Sargent's Sons Corp
Production control systems	Plessey	Telecontrol
Protective packaging	Jiffy Packaging	Jiffy Manufacturing
Pulp and paper equipment	Millspaugh	Modern Machines
Pumps and associated equipment	David Brown	Bingham Pump Co
	Zwicky	Viking Pump
	Gener l Engineering; Integral	New York Air Brake Co
	Cockburns	De Laval Turbine
	*Sigmund Pulsometer Pumps	Airbanks Morse, Division of Colt Industries
Pumps (axial flow)	GEC	Morris Machine Works
Pumps (hydraulic)	Wallwork Gears	S C Carter Co Inc
Pumps (oil burner)	Lee Howl	Webster Electric Co
	International Paper Single Service	Ex-Cell-O Corp
Pumps, valves and cylinders	Rubery Owen	Hydraulic Unit Specialities
Pure-Pak	International Paper Single Service	Ex-Cell-O Corp
Railway equipment	Rootes Pressings	Chesapeake & Ohio Railway

*indicates cross-licensing agreement

Product	Licensee	Licensor
Railway maintenance equipment	Stracham & Henshaw	Whiting Corp
Reed switches	Flight Refuelling	Hamlin
Refinery fittings	Lake & Elliott	ACF Industries
Refinery fittings and castings	APV-Paramount	Sivyer Steel Casting
Refractories	Morgan Refractories	Emhart Corp
Refractory, heat-insulating fibre	Morganite Ceramic Fibres	Babcock & Wilcox (New York)
Refrigerating systems	Winget	Dole Refrigerating Co
Refrigeration equipment	L Sterne	Tecumseh Products
Refuse incineration plant	West's (Manchester)	Takuma Boiler Manufacturing (Japan)
Regulators	Clyde Blowers	Leslie Co
Relays and stepping switches	Elliott-Automation	C P Clare & Co
Resistors	Welwyn Electric	Vishay Instrument
Retaining rings	Wellworthy	Ramsey Corp
Road machinery	Aveling-Barford	Baldwin-Lima-Hamilton Corp (Construction Equipment Division Austin-Western Plant)
Rolling mills and processing equipment	Loewy Robertson	T Sendzimir; Torrington Manufacturing
Rolling mills, combustion control equipment	Davy & United Engineering	Morgan Construction Co
Rotary die cutting machinery	Henry Simon	L E Sauer Machine Co
Rotary engines	Rolls-Royce	NSU/Wankel
Rotex screeners	Locker Industries	The Orville Simpson Co
Rotor gyros	Elliott-Automation	North American Aviation

*indicates cross-licensing agreement

Product	Licensee	Licensor
Rubber and plastics machinery	Francis Shaw	Spadone Machine; McNeil Corp; American Biltrite Rubber Farrel Corp; NRM Corp
	David Bridge	
	BTR Industries	Resistoflex
Rubber tyre couplings	Sheepbridge Engineering	Findusco (Switzerland)
Scaffolding	Access Equipment	UP-Right Scaffolds
	Alexander Shanks	Union Metal
Scales, weight recorders and systems	Henry Simon	Howe Richardson Scale
Screened enclosures	Belling & Lee	Filtron
Screens and screening equipment	International Combustion	W S Tyler
Screw machines	BSA Electrics	National Acme
Screws	Linread	Continental Screw
	CAV; Rolls-Royce	Standard Screw Co
Self cleaning strainers	Royles	Adams Co
Semiconductor devices, integrated circuits	Elliott-Automation	Fairchild Camera & Instrument
	Thorn Electric	International Rectifier Corp
Sems units	Crane's Screw & Colygrip Castor	Illinois Tool Works
Servo components	*Moore, Reed	Vernitron Corp
Shearing machines	Oliver Machinery	Blue Valley Machine & Manufacturing
Sheet metal machinery	Oliver Machinery	Dreis & Krump Manufacturing
Sheet metal working equipment	Head Wrightson	Stamco
Ship unloaders	Ashmore, Benson, Pease	Dravo Corp
Shock absorbers	Armstrong Patents	Resources & Facilities

*indicates cross-licensing agreement

Product	Licensee	Licensor
Shock and vibration equipment	Cementation (Muffelite)	Barry Controls Division, Barry Wright
Shoes	Sexton, Son & Everard Somervell Bros Saxone, Lilley & Skinner British Shoe Corp	Joyce United States Shoe Corp Vaisey Bristol Shoe Wolverine World Wide
Shuttle kilns	Gibbons Brothers	Denver Fireclay
Silverware	Betts	International Silver
Slip rings, relays, switches	IDM Electronics	Electro-Tec
Sludge thickening equipment	Simon Engineering	Licencia (Hungary)
Small and miniature motors, gearheads	Plessey	Rowe Industries
Solenoids, switches, relays, step-servo motors, rectifiers and arc suppressors	NSF	Ledex
Solenoids, transformers, relays	Plessey	Dormeyer Industries
Sorting equipment (automated)	Bagshawe & Co	Speaker Sortation Systems
Spectrophotometers	Hilger & Watts	Guildford Instrument Labs
Spray drying equipment	L A Mitchell	Bowen Engineering
Spring control of piping systems	Vokes	Bergen Pipesupport
Stainless steel containers	Fairey Engineering	Firestone Tire & Rubber
Stainless steel fabrications	Delaney Gallay	Stainless Steel Products
Stainless steel products	A Johnson	Surface Separator Systems; Votator Division, Chemetron
Steam turbine engines	Hayward Tyler	Terry Steam Turbine
Steel and aluminium doors	RTZ Metals	Alumiline Corp

*indicates cross-licensing agreement

Product	Licensee	Licensor
Steel castings	APV-Paramount	Esco International
Steel coil handling equipment	B Thornton	Braner Engineering
Steel manufacturing processes	Steel Company of Wales	Yawata Steel (Japan); Toyo Kohan (Japan)
Steel plate, tank fabrications	Whessoe	Chicago Bridge & Iron Co
Steel processing equipment	Albright & Wilson; Head Wrightson Richardson, Westgarth	National Steel Corp Krupps (West Germany)
Steel scaffolding	Sterling Foundry Specialists	Safway Steel Products
Steel structural products	Tecalemit Capper-Neill; Wm Neill	Reynolds Manufacturing Pittsburgh–Des Moines Steel Co
Storage tanks	Whessoe	General Precision
Storage tanks, steel fabrications	Frederick Braby	Columbian Steel Tank
Strain gauge accessories, instrumentation	Welwyn Electric Mawdsley's	W T Bean Ramapo Instrument
Stress measures	Horstham	Photolastic
String tying machines	Sheridan Machinery	B H Bunn
Switches	Plessey Painton NSF	Illinois Tool Works Donald P Mossman Eaton Yale & Towne
Switches (thumb wheel)	Plessey	Electronic Engineering
Switchgear, scientific	Venner	Rockwell Manufacturing; Yardney International Corp
Swivel joints, loading arms, valves	Oil Well Engineering: Hindle Valves	Chiksan Division FMC
Synthetic fibre and paper insulation	Langley London	Rogers Corp

*indicates cross-licensing agreement

Product	Licensee	Licensor
Systems and components for missiles, aircraft and space projection	Plessey	Whittaker Corp
Tank cleaning machines	Samuel Hodge	Pyrate Sales
Tap and screw gauges	Mercer & Garside	Besly-Welles
Taper leaf springs	Bramber Engineering	Rockwell-Standard
Telecine and slide scanning equipment	EMI	Thomson Houston (France)
Telecommunication equipment	Elliott-Automation; Plessey	Western Electric
Telephone and telegraph terminal equipment	Racal Electronics	Tele-Signal Corp
Television transmitting aerial panels	Racal Electronics	Rhode & Schwarz (West Germany)
Temperature and pressure controls	*Elliott-Automation Chamberlain & Hookham	Robertshaw Controls
Textile machinery	*Prince-Smith & Stells	Mitsubishi (Japan)
Textiles	J Chadwick	Deering Milliken Research
	Qualitex Yarns	Spunize Co of America
Thermo-forming machinery	Davy Plastics Machinery	Bocchi (Italy)
Thermoplastic adhesives	Cray Valley Products	General Mills
Time control systems	Bruce Peebles Industries; Edgcumbe Peebles; Everett Edgcumbe	Automatic Timing & Control
Tobacco processing machinery	Vokes Group	Cardwell Machine Co
Toiletries and pharmaceuticals	Paines & Byrne	Nestle LeMur

*indicates cross-licensing agreement

Product	Licensee	Licensor
Torque converters	Rolls-Royce	Twin Disc Clutch Co
Tower cranes	Pearson Machine Tool	EWK (West Germany)
Transfer machinery	Thomas Ryder	H R Krueger
Transistors, diodes and rectifiers	Plessey	General Instrument Corp
Transmissions, clutches, gears	Rolls-Royce Robinson Campbell	Twin Disc Clutch Co; General Motors Toutechnique (France)
Transportation, bulk handling, plastics etc.	Albright & Wilson; Power Gas	General American Transportation
Transportation equipment	Cravens Homalloy	Strick Corp
Trouser belts	Clutsom & Kemp	Le Cottier (France)
Trouser waistbands and linings	H G Graham	Ban-Rol Co
Truck dumper	Simon-Barron	Screw Conveyor
Trucks (industrial)	Brush Electrical Engineering	Barrett-Cravens
Trucks (hydraulic tipping)	Warwick Production	Wilhelm Gmohling (West Germany)
Tubing (Teflon)	Uni-Tubes	Titeflex
Turbines and allied equipment	Centrax	North American Rockwell
Turbo chargers	Holset Engineering Dowty	Wallace-Murray Garrett
Tyre reconditioning	Vacu-Lug Traction Tyre	Bacon American Corp
Tyre remoulding equipment	Henry W Peabody	Ransburg Electro-Coating
Ultrasonic cleaning equipment	Radyne	Westinghouse Electric
Ultrasonic cleaning equipment, instruments, hi fi sound systems	Elliott Bros (London)	Acoustica Associates

*indicates cross-licensing agreement

Product	Licensee	Licensor
Ultrasonic spot welding equipment	Kerry's (Ultrasonics)	Sonobond Corp
Ultrasonic testing equipment	Watson & Sons; Smiths Industries	Automation Industries
	Dawe Instruments	Branson Instruments
Urea production plant	Woodall-Duckham ICI	Snam Progetti (Italy) Toyo Koatsu (Japan)
Vacuum alarm glass	Mann-Reddington Group	Securiton (Switzerland)
Valves	J Blakeborough George Clark & Sons (Hull) NSF Jamesbury-Serck Wellman Controls Audco Newman, Hender; Cockburns Weir-Pacific Valves Telehoist	Atwood & Morrill American Machine & Foundry Dole Valve Co Jamesbury Corp Ross Operating Valve Borsig (West Germany) Rockwell Manufacturing Autoclave Engineers Koehring
Valves and automatic process control equipment	Crosby Valve & Engineering; Serck Glocon Hymatic Engineering	Worthington Control Kieley & Mueller
Valves, automatic control equipment, plastic products	Laycock Engineering	Hays Manufacturing
Valves, consistency regulators	Millspaugh	DeZurik Corp
Valves (ball)	Audco English Electric	Borsig AG (West Germany) Netherton & Cook Valve Co
Valves (control)	Elliott-Automation	Devar-Kinetics Division CEC
Valves (oil)	Joshua Hindle	General Valve
Valves (safety relief)	Elliott-Automation; Farris Engineering	Farris Engineering

*indicates cross-licensing agreement

Product	Licensee	Licensor
Valves (water)	*Plessey*	*Nostorag (Switzerland)*
Vegetable oil	*Younghusband, Stephens*	*Pacific Vegetable Oil Corp*
Vehicles	*Rolls-Royce*	*General Motors*
Vehicles (custom built)	*Winget*	*Mack Trucks*
Vending machinery	*Fisher & Ludlow*	*National Vendors*
Venetian blinds	*Home Fittings*	*Kirsch*
Ventilating equipment	*Ozonair* *Solar Controlair*	*Air Balance* *Swartwout Fabricators*
Versatron programmed positioning and handling automation	*Hawker Siddeley Dynamics*	*American Machine & Foundry*
Vibratory materials handling automation equipment	*Riley (IC) Products*	*Syntron*
Vibrating screens and crushers	*Griffiths Bentley*	*Appareils Dragon (France)*
Video studio equipment	*Autonetics*	*International Interface*
Vinyl foam	*Elson & Robbins*	*Girdler Process Equipment*
Vinyl products processing	*Oak Rubber*	*Sun Rubber Corp*
Water softening equipment	*Young Chemical Engineering*	*Culligan International*
Water coolers and filters	*Crawley Bros*	*Sunroc Corp*
Water cooling towers, air cooled heat exchangers	*Heenan & Froude*	*Marley Co*
Welding and metal forming equipment	*Hall Engineering*	*Delta Welder Corp*
Welding cables	*Haddon Cables*	*Mackworth Rees Division, Avis Industrial*
Welding equipment	*Marshall Richards Machine*	*Stryco Manufacturing*

*indicates cross-licensing agreement

Product	Licensee	Licensor
Welding plant (electric)	*Murex Welding Processes*	*Chemetron Corp*
Welding plant (heavy-duty)	*A I Welders*	*Guild Metal Joining Equipment*
Welding positioners, turning rolls	*Murex Positioning Equipment*	*Aronson Machine*
Wire drawing and cable machinery	*Joseph Winterburn Winget Syncro*	*Berlyn Corp Syncro Machine*
Wire drawing equipment and machinery	*Reliance Gear*	*Coulter & McKenzie*
Writing equipment	*Joseph Gillott*	*Hunt Manufacturing*
Z blade mixers	*Premier Colloid Mills*	*Ateliers de Construction Mechaniques y Guittard (France)*

*indicates cross-licensing agreement

18
OTHER MANUFACTURING INDUSTRIES

In the area of process plant and mechanical engineering, the leading American-owned companies are Kellogg, Bechtel, Foster Wheeler and the Fluor Corporation. Kellogg International, whose parent company is Pullman of Chicago, has £84 million of overseas projects in hand. Bechtel, whose head office is in San Francisco, specialises in refineries building. Foster Wheeler, with a parent company in New Jersey, specialises in petroleum and petrochemical plant and also makes water-tube boilers, process heating equipment and a range of heavy-duty supplies. Fluor is one of the world's largest chemical engineering construction groups. Its headquarters are in Los Angeles and it runs offices in London and Holland. The group is currently building the largest hydrocracker plant in Europe for BP at Grangemouth. Other large manufacturers of chemical engineering plant, all American owned, include Procon, Ralph M Parsons, Dorr-Oliver, Chemical Construction and Catalytic International. All these companies are engaged in extensive overseas work.

American Machine & Foundry Company of New York has a Belfast subsidiary, AMF Beaird, which manufactures storage tanks for the oil, gas and petrochemical industries of Europe. Later in its development the company plans to extend its manufacturing capacity to include road tankers, delivery trucks, specially designed tanks for refinery and industrial plants and cryogenic storage tanks.

Rockwell Manufacturing, the leading American supplier of measurement and control equipment bought a 20 per cent share in United Gas Industries in the early part of 1968, with an option on a further 15 per cent which it intends to exercise. UGI is active in gas control and measuring equipment. Rockwell has stated that it has no plans to enlarge its share of UGI beyond 35 per cent, but it has made no secret of the fact that it is sounding out other companies which might be interested in coming under its control.

In October 1968 the British Oxygen Company and Air Reduction of the US formed a joint venture to manufacture and market cryogenic and other process plant on both sides of the Atlantic. The London concern is called BOC/AIRCO; the New Jersey end is AIRCO/BOC. Air Products, whose parent company is in Pennsylvania is another leading manufacturer of industrial gases and process plant.

Hooker Chemical, an American group which recently merged with Occidental Petroleum, recently made a bid for the 75 per cent it does not already own of Efco, the company which has interests in heat treatment furnaces, electroplating equipment and solutions.

The Swedish Oltronix is setting up a factory in Hitchin for the production of its range of stabilised power supply units. The firm manufactures over 100 types of unit, until recently it only maintained a sales representation in the UK. Brush Clevite, part of the Clevite Corporation of the US is to increase its production capacity at Southampton by 60 per cent. The company, in which the Charterhouse Group has a ten per cent stake, has acquired from Plessey a major shareholding in Technical Ceramics of Swindon, the remainder of the equity of this company being held by another American – Sonotone. Brush Clevite is now Europe's largest producer of piezoelectric ceramics used in pick-up cartridges.

The GHH Group of Oberhausen in Western Germany, active in machinery and steel manufacture, has set up a British subsidiary.

Rationalisation of manufacturing in a British and a West German company which could also set a trend in future co-operation has been announced recently. The agreement is between Enots of Birmingham, specialists in pneumatic and lubrication equipment and the Berlin firm Willy Vogel which produces an extensive range of centralised lubrication equipment. The ultimate aim is to do away with duplication and in due course Enots will drop all centralised lubrication equipment development, while Vogel will cease work on new pneumatic equipment. Enots has the sole selling rights for Vogel lubrication products in the UK and Commonwealth; Vogel is the agent for Enots pneumatic products in Germany.

The scientific instruments field is another diverse sphere of operations, a number of concerns active in electronics also manufacture instruments. British companies, such as Cambridge Instrument and George Kent rely to a greater or lesser extent on licensing agreements, particularly with the large American companies. The Philips subsidiaries are also important through Pye Unicam and MEL Equipment, which is now merging with Pye Unicam following the Philips/Pye rationalisation of interests. American owned Hewlett Packard specialises in measuring instruments and manufactures more than 1500 types. It has an active British division in Slough.

One of the chief suppliers of laboratory equipment is Quickfit & Quartz, a subsidiary of James Jobling which is 40 per cent owned by Corning Glass of New York. Quickfit exports 43 per cent of its total output and is a winner of a Queen's award for export performance.

Air-Shields (UK) with a Pennsylvania parent is important in specialised medical equipment which is the province of a number of US-owned concerns. Dylade of London is owned by Milton Roy of Florida; Dylade makes artificial kidney machines and is currently testing prototypes of a cheap and compact heat sterilising machine.

Bausch & Lomb is one of the largest companies making optical components and a range of scientific instruments. The American Optical Corp of Massachusetts is a leading manufacturer of ophthalmic equipment, scientific instruments and electro-medical equipment. Its British subsidiary is British American Optical which also manufactures diamond tools and abrasives. American Optical is now part of Warner-Lambert Pharmaceutical.

Bard-Davol, whose parent company is in New Jersey, manufactures urological and special medical instruments; S H Camp makes surgical appliances at its Northern Ireland factory while the parent company is in Michigan. Brunswick Corporation, which also has a factory in Northern Ireland, manufactures hypodermic syringes and other medical instruments. Its head office is in Chicago. S S White of Phildaelphia has a Harrow subsidiary; Zimmer Orthopaedic is another American company in the medical field.

The remaining companies which are controlled to a greater or less degree by overseas interests and which have not been mentioned in preceding chapters are listed below.

Mining & oilfield equipment

British company	Product range	Parent company
B H & H Services (distribute in UK for parent company and act as representatives for a number of other American interests)	oilfield equipment	Beckley, Haltom & Hickman Services, New Jersey
Baker Oil Tools	drilling, production and completion equipment	Baker Oil Tools, California
Black, Sivalls & Bryson	oil production equipment	Black, Sivalls & Bryson, Kansas City
Burden Drilling & Pipeline Contractors	pipeline systems	O R Burden Construction Corp, Oklahoma

British company	Product range	Parent company
Camco	oilfield equipment	Camco Inc, Houston
Cameron Iron Works	oilfield equipment	Cameron Iron Works, Houston
Eimco	mining and tunnelling machinery, vacuum filtration, water waste and sewage treatment equipment	Eimco Corp, Salt Lake City
Halliburton	oilfield equipment and oilwell services	Halliburton, Oklahoma
Hughes Tool	oil drilling rock bits	Hughes Tool, Houston
Joy Manufacturing	mining machinery, air compressors, pneumatic tools, rock and core drills, conveyor rollers	Joy Manufacturing, Pittsburgh
Mission Manufacturing	oilfield equipment	Mission Manufacturing, Houston
National Supply	oilfield machinery	National Supply Division of Armco Steel (Houston)

Scientific instruments

British company	Product range	Parent company
AEP International	electronic instruments and components	AEP International Canada
Analytical Measurements	electrometers	Analytical Measurements Inc, New Jersey
Applied Research Laboratories (GB)	scientific instruments	Bausch & Lomb, New York
BFI Electronics	electronic instruments and equipment	B Freudenberg, New York
Baird-Atomic	analysers, instruments and equipment	Baird-Atomic, Massachusetts
Beckman Instruments	precision electrical instruments	Beckman Instruments, California
Becton, Dickinson UK	medical and surgical instruments	Becton, Dickinson, New Jersey
Brooks Instrument	industrial instruments	Emerson Electric, Pennsylvania
Cahn Instrument	scientific instruments	Cahn Instrument, California
Coulter Electronics	electronic instruments, laboratory equipment	Coulter Electronics, Florida
Derritron Group	industrial electronic equipment	AGAC-Derritron
Endevco	instrumentation, transducers, equipment for environmental testing	Endevco, Pasadena
Fischer & Porter	process control instrumentation	Fischer & Porter, Pennsylvania
Foxborough-Yoxall	industrial instruments	Foxboro Co, Massachusetts
Instro	precision materials testing instruments	Instron Corp, Massachusetts
C E Johansson	screw thread products, metrology instruments	AB Svenska Kullagerfabriken, Sweden

British company	Product range	Parent company
Kistler Instruments	piezoelectric measuring instruments, transducers, accelerometers, amplifiers	Kistler Instrumente AG, Switzerland
LTV-Ling Altec	electronic equipment and systems, vibration testing equipment	Ling-Temko-Vought, Dallas
Lloyd & Hillman	industrial instruments and accessories	Pall Corp, New York
Mica	glass fibre boards for printed circuits	Mica Corp, California
Neptune Meter	industrial meters	joint subsidiary of Parkinson Cowan and Neptune Measurement, New York
Ocli Optical Coatings	infra-red filters, optical coatings	Optical Coating Laboratory, California
Ovee Spring Gauge	screw and thread gauges	Ovee Gauge Co, California
Parkinson Cowan Compteurs	integrated system design, advisory and equipment testing and supply service for measurement control in the gas industry	joint subsidiary of Parkinson Cowan and Compagnie des Compteurs, France
Ranco Controls	temperature controls, heating equipment, motors, accessories	Ranco Inc, Ohio
Sahlin Engineering	automation equipment	Sahlin Engineering, Michigan
Seismograph Service	geophysical survey equipment	Seismograph, Oklahoma
Spectra-Physics	gas lasers	Spectra-Physics, California
Technicon Instruments	scientific instruments	Technicon International, New York

British company	Product range	Parent company
Varian Associates	*microwave tubes, spectrometers, linear accelerators, vacuum products*	*Varian Associates, California*
Veeder-Root	*counting, indicating, controlling, recording and computing instruments*	*Veder-Root, Connecticut*
Wallace & Tiernan	*chemical process control equipment*	*Wallace & Tiernan, New Jersey*

Metallurgy (ferrous and non-ferrous) and metal products

British company	Product range	Parent company
Alpha Metals	*high purity and semi-conductor preforms and solder products*	*Alpha Metals Inc, Jersey City*
Armco	*steel and steel products, equipment, machines*	*Armco Steel Corp, Ohio*
Centrax-Misco	*investment castings*	*Howmet, New York*
Chicago Bridge	*steel plate fabrication*	*Chicago Bridge & Iron, Illinois*
Clyde Tube Forgings	*forgings, pipe fittings*	*Chemetron Corp, Chicago*
Crusteel	*special steels*	*Crucible Steel Co, Pittsburgh*
Enthoven & Sons	*lead smelting and refining*	*NV Billiton Maatschappij (Netherlands)*
Eutectic Welding Alloys	*welding supplies*	*Eutectic Corp, New York*
George Fischer (GB) and two subsidiaries: Le Bas Tube; Britannia Iron & Steel Works	*malleable iron tube fittings and castings*	*George Fischer AG (Switzerland)*

British company	Product range	Parent company
Hoganas	powder metallurgy	Hoganas (Sweden)
Holo-Krome	socket screws	Veeder-Root, Connecticut
C H Johnson	metal products, machinery and equipment	Johnson Wire Works, Canada
Kaiser Le Nickel	nickel	owned jointly by Kaiser Aluminium & Chemical Corp, California and Société Le Nickel of France
Pernix Ethone	surface treatments for metals and plastics	American Smelting & Refining, New York
Raychem	wire products	joint subsidiary of Bakelite Xylonite and Raychem Corp of California
Sandusky	centrifugal castings	Sandusky Foundry & Machine Co, Ohio
Signode	steel strapping equipment	Signode Corp, Chicago
Taylor Stainless Metals	steel stockholdings	Nyby Stainless Steels (Sweden)
Torrington Co	roller bearings, needles, screws, wire wheel components	Torrington Co, Connecticut
George Tucker Eyelet	light metal pressings	United Shoe Machinery Corp
Uddeholm	Swedish steels, strip, wire rods, tubes etc	Uddeholm (Sweden)
Unbrako	alloy steel bars and wire, precision fasteners etc	Standard Pressed Steel, Pennsylvania
Whitecroft-Scovill	wire goods	Scovill Manufacturing, Connecticut

Specialised plant and machinery

British company	Product range	Parent company
Ajax Magnathermic	induction melting and heating equipment	Ajax Magnathermic Corp, Ohio
American Air Filter GB	air filter and dust control equipment	American Air Filter, Kentucky
Appleco Europe	chillers, cooling towers, water recovery plant	Applications Engineering, Illinois
Arenco-Alite	precision filling machines	Arenco AB, Sweden
Badger	chemical and petroleum plant engineering and construction	Badger Co, Massachusetts
Henry Balfour	gas and chemical plant, pressure vessels and castings	Ritter Pfaudler, New York
Balzers High Vacuum	vacuum plant and components	Werkzeugsmachinen-fabrik, Oerlikon Bührle (Switzerland)
Band-It Co	industrial pressure clamps	Band-It Co, Denver
Big Drum Equipment	machinery and packaging for ice cream	Big Drum Inc, Ohio
Big Dutchman GB	automatic poultry and livestock industry equipment	Big Dutchman Inc, Michigan
E W Bliss (England)	power press and can-making machinery	E W Bliss, Ohio
C F Braun	petroleum, chemical and metallurgical plant	C F Braun, California
British Ceca	solvent recovery plant, gas drying equipment, dust collectors	Ceca, France
Broughton UK	ancillary equipment for paper machines	Broughton Corp, New York
Burgess-Manning	noise dampening equipment	Burgess-Manning, Dallas

British company	Product range	Parent company
Cardox GB	non-explosive blasting equipment and high pressure air systems	Marmon-Harrington, Indiana
Cincinnati Shaper	guillotine shears and press brakes	Cincinnati Shaper, Ohio
Constantin (Engineers)	chemical processing and water treatment plant; cement-making machinery; bulk materials handling	General American Transportation Corp, Chicago
Cooper-Bessemer UK	engines and compressors	Cooper Industries, Ohio
John Dalglish & Sons	industrial drying and cloth finishing machinery	Proctor-Silex Corp, Pennsylvania
Diamond Power Speciality	boiler cleaning equipment	Diamond Power Speciality, Ohio
Hayssen Manufacturing	automatic wrapping and packaging machinery	Hayssen Manufacturing, Wisconsin
Hull Corporation	plastics machinery, encapsulation and vacuum equipment, food processing machinery	Hull Corp, Pennyslvania
Ipsen Industries	heat treating equipment	Ipsen Industries, Illinois
Lavino (Machinery)	grinding and classifying machines (sales)	Onival Corp, Philadelphia
Metco	metal and ceramic flame spraying equipment	Metco, New York
McKee Process Machinery	process machinery for textiles and plastics	Arthur G McKee, Cleveland
Geo J Meyer	packaging equipment	Geo J Meyer Manufacturing, Wisconsin
Millspaugh	paper and board making machinery	Escher Wyss, Zurich
Mine Safety Appliances	industrial safety equipment	Mine Safety Appliances, Pittsburgh

British company	Product range	Parent company
Morse Controls	marine and industrial control systems	Morse Controls, Ohio
Pennsalt	centrifugal processing equipment, plastic moulding, tabletting presses, high vacuum equipment, grinding equipment, metal processing	Pennsalt Chemicals, Philadelphia
Petrolite	chemical and electrical processing equipment	Petrolite Corp, St Louis
Rubery, Owen-Drott	mechanical handling systems	Drott Manufacturing Corp, Milwaukee
Salem-Brosius	industrial furnaces	Salem-Brosius, Pennsylvania
Sheppard & Sons	scrap processing plant and ingot casting machines	American Hoist & Derrick, Minnesota
Society Genevoise	jig boring machines, measuring machines, projectors etc	Societe Genevoise d'Instruments de Physique, Geneva
Turner Machinery	leather and plastics machinery	United Shoe Machinery Corp, Boston
Vacu-Blast	shot blasting machinery	Vacu-Blast, California
Vaughn-Crossley	wire drawing, cutting, galvanizing, patenting and winding machinery	Vaughn Machinery, Ohio
John Zink	Combustion equipment	John Zink, Oklahoma

It is both tempting and easy to lose a sense of proportion when carrying out an across-the-board investigation of this nature; easy to ignore the major contributions made by the all-British companies; tempting to talk of the overseas take-over of industry. Inevitably this comes down to the wide spread of American interests and perhaps the following chart, produced by the us Department of Commerce and reproduced from the First National Bank of Chicago's monthly bulletin (May 1968) will help to put this aspect into perspective.

Flow of direct investment funds to Western Europe

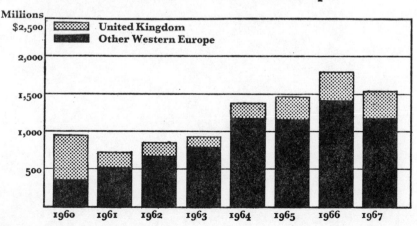

The increase in business capital investment flows to western Europe in recent years has, in fact, been concentrated in nations other than the UK, mainly the Common Market countries. American money and know-how is an important contribution, but compared with the total overseas investment pattern of American industry, the British sector is but a small proportion of their world-wide operations.

A glance at the *Times* latest annual review of leading companies shows only four of the top 20 listed foreign controlled in any way. These companies are Shell, Unilever, Esso and Ford; add F W Woolworth and we find that the list can be extended to cover the top 50. Even so, Shell and Unilever have almost as much British as overseas capital invested in them. Neither have we taken into consideration the outward investments by British companies, which is another story.

Perhaps the one lesson we can learn is the tremendous impact made by the foreign-owned companies as a result of their dynamic marketing and, of course, by their skilled use of public relations. There is no black magic in the fact that when a foreign-owned concern wishes to penetrate a market sector it is usually successful in gaining its estimated share in the shortest possible time.